THREE-WEEK PROFESSIONALS

THREE-WEEK PROFESSIONALS

INSIDE THE 1987 NFL PLAYERS' STRIKE

Ted Kluck

ROWMAN & LITTLEFIELD
Lanham • Boulder • New York • London

Published by Rowman & Littlefield
A wholly owned subsidary of The Rowman & Littlefield Publishing Group, Inc.
4501 Forbes Boulevard, Suite 200, Lanham, Maryland 20706
www.rowman.com

Unit A, Whitacre Mews, 26-34 Stannary Street, London SE11 4AB

British Library Cataloguing in Publication Information Available

Library of Congress Cataloging-in-Publication Data

Kluck, Ted.
Three-week professionals : inside the 1987 NFL players' strke / Ted Kluck.
pages cm
Includes bibliographical references and index.
ISBN 978-1-4422-4154-1 (hardcover : alk. paper) -- ISBN 978-1-4422-4155-8 (ebook)
1. National Football League—History—20th century. 2. Football—United States—History—20th century. 3. Strikes and lockouts—United States—History—20th century. 4. Strikebreakers—United States—History—20th century. 5. Football players—Labor unions—United States. 6. Football players—Salaries, etc.—United States. I. Title.
GV955.5.N35K58 2015
796.332'64—dc23
2015008197

∞™ The paper used in this publication meets the minimum requirements of American National Standard for Information Sciences Permanence of Paper for Printed Library Materials, ANSI/NISO Z39.48-1992.

Printed in the United States of America

For all of the football players

CONTENTS

ACKNOWLEDGMENTS

This book was a joy. It was a joy because it involved delving into football, into my childhood, and into relationships with people whose stories I care about.

I was encouraged (and the book was made possible) by the graciousness of the men who sat for interviews for this project: Joe Bock, whom I played against in a low-rent arena league; Mike Hohensee and Mike Hold, who distinguished themselves in the "big" arena league (the Arena Football League [AFL]) as coaches and players; guys like John Reaves and Steve Dils, who were NFL quarterbacks turned leaders in their industries; Bill Maas, who is a nose tackle turned television commentator; Al Wolden, who is a replacement running back turned schoolteacher and family man; Leigh Steinberg, who is a super agent turned regular guy turned super agent again; doctors like Robert Fabiano and Robert Cantu; Dr. Ron Calhoun, a turf grass expert; Keith Butler, who was a Seattle Seahawks linebacker turned defensive coordinator for the Pittsburgh Steelers; Larry Linne, wide receiver turned entrepreneur; Adrian Breen, quarterback turned bank president; Les Steckel, who is a Marine turned football coach turned ministry leader; and Jeff Kemp, who is the son of a congressman turned ministry leader himself.

Special thanks to Christen Karniski from Rowman & Littlefield, who championed this project, and to Kristin Kluck, my wife, for her steadfast patience, kindness, and encouragement (and long-suffering through years and years of football). And to the shadowy Internet figure who supplied my game DVDs.

Final thanks go to Tristan and Maxim, my sons, for watching the games with me. You guys are the best.

PROLOGUE

Here I Go Again: Football in France

It feels good to have pads on again. It's been several years. After landing in Dublin and waiting a few hours, we connected to Paris.

One of the most interesting features of the Charles De Gaulle Airport is the elaborate tunnel system that connects one floor to another. The tunnel configuration feels very 1950s-mod George Jetson. We waited a few more hours in Paris before riding the train from Paris to Rennes, which broke down and sat on the tracks for ninety minutes. During this time, the train was completely dark, and the conductor was making announcements over the loudspeaker, none of which we could understand because of the usual tinny loudspeaker dynamic and also because it was in French. In front of us, a French mother sat with her children, who were both about our boys' age. She turned around and offered her cell phone, on which she had called her husband who spoke fluent English. He translated for us, and after the lights came back on she whipped around and began regaling us with conversation in her own broken English. Within minutes our kids were watching movies and playing video games together, which would permanently dispel the notion that all French people (1) hate Americans and (2) are snobby and aloof. This first notion would be dispelled often and actually in six-ish weeks; the other notion would never be proven. Eight hours after landing in Dublin, we finally arrived in St. Brieuc, where we were greeted by the Hosdez family.

Two years ago, I contacted Jean-Michel Hosdez, owner of the St. Brieuc Licornes American Football Club via email, and pitched him on my strange idea of a writing retreat in France, during which I would be playing and coaching for his team and writing in some way, shape, or form about the experience. He wrote back almost immediately, setting in motion what would become a beautiful email-based friendship between our wives and would be the beginning of a football journey for us.

Football practice is held in a small soccer stadium on the outskirts of Saint Brieuc overlooking St. Brieuc Bay, which is a part of the English Channel. To say that it's the most beautiful place in which I've ever had a football practice would be a massive understatement. In fact, while warming up and doing drills on the pristine field turf, I find myself glancing out over the bay and looking around me at the beautiful sixteenth-century stone buildings where people live and work. It occurs to me that people spend a couple of hundred bucks and a couple of days sweating through replicas of these streets in places like Disney World or the Epcot Center. Today, I'm living it.

As a group, this team is classier than any semipro team I was ever a part of in America. I jog around the field with Arnaud, a wide receiver who, when he isn't playing football, is a database administrator for a company that sells organic turkeys. Jean-Mi, the owner and a part-time offensive guard, works in the mayor's office in a nearby tourist town called Pleneuf. Our best wide receiver is also an oral surgeon. They are, to a man, warm, kind, and interested in me. The practice is a success—I catch balls, hit guys, and feel great—and I'm euphoric, if not a little jet lagged.

Being back in the orb of football is a reminder of one of my fantasies but also one of my greatest areas of sin. I basically want to be everyone's hero. Even at my advanced age I want to be the guy who comes in, has one practice, and then single-handedly manages to turn around the fortunes of the Licornes in one shot. I want to sack quarterbacks and score touchdowns on Sunday. I basically want to be the football hero that God has never really allowed me to be . . . probably because it wouldn't do me any good, spiritually, to be this kind of hero. Still, I want it.

The bus ride to Caen will be nearly three hours. In the cold frost of morning we gathered at Jean-Mi's house, drove to the bus terminal, and loaded our gear into the belly of the bus. A linebacker, Jann, has brought his girlfriend and his father. She greets us with the traditional French "bonjour" and a kiss on the cheek. She later offers candy and hot chocolate to the boys. This will not be the bus ride of my semi-pro past, fueled by beer, strip clubs, and lewd conversation. I snuggle in next to Tristan, sharing my iPod earbuds, and we both listen to music and both, probably, dream of football glory.

I have no business dreaming of this. I'm too old, and too, probably, out of shape. Even though I've done my best to get in shape my body is defying me. It looks worse than it did six years ago when I played in a low-rent arena league, and worse than two years ago when I played semi-pro in the Lansing area. Despite my best efforts, my body is failing me and entropy is taking over. It frustrates me to no end. Still, I dream.

My teammates dream, too, which is, the older I get, I think, the point of football at all—it gives us all something to dream about. I find out that Max, our running back, and Pac, our best guard, both started playing football because they were so moved by the movie *Friday Night Lights*. Max has even read the book in English.

"You didn't get bogged down in the history of Odessa and all that stuff?" I ask.

"No, I loved it," he replies.

He and Pac have seen every American football movie ever made, from *Rudy* to *The Replacements*, which should be alternately titled *The End of Keanu Reeves's Career*.

I find out that Cammie, our starting cornerback, used to be a national champion amateur kickboxer in France. "But I am afraid to tackle," he says, sweetly and honestly. "Do you have any advices [sic]?"

In America, this would never happen. A football player in America would never admit to being afraid of anything, which creates the culture of chest-thumping false bravado that has ruined so many football experiences.

Mont. St. Michel, a famous abbey, goes by in the distance, and my English-speaking friend Arnaud helpfully points it out. As we enter Caen, I see signs for Normandy beach memorials and historic sites. I see beautiful buildings. I feel, in my stomach, the familiar and particular feeling of pregame nerves that I have felt every pregame since I first played organized football at age nine. I feel, also, like vomiting. I can only imagine what the guys tumbling out of those boats onto the Normandy beaches must have felt.

The locker room feels familiar. Guys undress in silence. Jerseys are passed out. Pregame rituals are upheld. Max, the running back for whom I'll be blocking, shows me how hammered and torn-up his jersey is, as a point of pride. I pull my jersey—number 43 in honor of my son who wore the same number this season—out of the plastic for the first time. I pull it over my pads. I smear greasepaint under my eyes. I check myself out in the mirror. These rituals know no cultural boundaries. Still, I have no idea how good the football is going to be here and assume I'll be among the best on the field. I am wrong. I am one of the best on *my* team, but our opponent is a different story altogether.

The Caen Conquerants are big, fast, strong, young, and extremely well-organized. Our team is a jolly band of misfits by comparison—we are the old (there are several players in their forties), the skinny (we have a cornerback who weighs 119 pounds), and the vastly inexperienced. It's apparent after about two series that the Conquerants would have run my small-college team off the field. On my first play, at fullback, I collide with their middle linebacker on an isolation play. He is around 260 pounds of pure, young, go-all-day fury, and I'll be colliding with him all day long. This is the stuff that concussions are made of.

The game atmosphere in Caen is weird. We don't really have fans except for a few family members and a cheerleading squad whose main function is to sit around, get photographed looking coquettish, and try and stay warm. There is no music, and the game takes place largely in relative silence, save for the crack of pads and the gasp of my own pained breathing.

How did we get here? While I'm in France basically playing for nothing, guys who are my age—like Tom Brady and Peyton Manning—will earn multiple millions piloting their teams in the NFL playoffs, which is far and away the biggest spectator event in American professional sports. Salaries and fan interest are both at all-time highs. In spite of player strikes in 1982 and 1987, and in spite of landmark free agency that has kept players on the move and changing teams, fans have never been more loyal and involved.

I cracked a rib in the second quarter and kept playing, and in fact, finished the game because, well, it's my last game. It hurts like crazy now. It hurts to laugh and bend over and cough and lie down and rise

up. It makes my already short fuse with my kids even shorter. The pain
of the game is the part that doesn't translate on television, no matter
how many high-definition cameras and talking heads are in the stadium.
Football is a savage game. It's hard to explain the satisfaction that
comes from playing it, which is part of what I'll explore with the 1987
replacement players, who played, largely, because it was an opportunity
to play one more time.

But when I shower and get dressed after the game and my teammates pat me on the shoulder and shake my hand, the handshakes and
shoulder pats are full of the kind of respect that only people who have
done this sort of thing can understand. They translate from culture to
culture, from border to border. And when I walk out into the cold night
air with my helmet in my hand and my hair wet from the shower, some
eye black still on my face, I feel . . . happy.

INTRODUCTION

Land of Confusion: Tape, Turf, and the NFL Players' Strike of 1987

In 2006, I was perhaps the worst professional football player in all of America. Let me explain. I was a long snapper and special teamer (technically also a linebacker and fullback) for the now-defunct Battle Creek Crunch of the surprisingly not-yet defunct Continental Indoor Football League (CIFL). We played for a few hundred bucks a game, often in front of only a few hundred people (despite official attendance figures in the thousands) in places like the Marion County War Memorial Coliseum (Marion, Ohio) and Kellogg Arena (Battle Creek, Michigan—"Cereal City USA!").

Still, it thrilled me to pull on a helmet, pull a shiny black jersey over my pads, and trot out onto old-school AstroTurf to play the "arena" version of American football on a short field with padded walls. The piped-in music was of the obligatory hip-hop variety, and my teammates had the obligatory minor league sad stories. One was a former All-American and NFL wide receiver who'd been cut by several teams. One flunked out of a Big Ten school where he had a scholarship. One, our kicker, was a pharmaceutical rep for a large drug company. Several, I think, were less-formal pharmaceutical reps.

I was benched halfway through the season as my once-perfect, like-clockwork long-snapping vanished in a haze of inexplicable anxiety, and I began skipping the ball off of the various turf surfaces we played on.

As a snapper, I lived with my head between my legs and saw the world upsidedown. As the snap skidded back, I would hear the groan from the audience, and then sometimes hear my kicker yelling, "Fire! Fire!" which is universal football language for, "There's been a bad snap, and I'm about to get killed." I would then turn and run—instinctively, like a school kid—after the football. Once, while doing this, I was blindsided by a member of the Marion (Ohio) Mayhem and went skidding, arm first, across the turf, losing a good bit of my skin in the process. I lost my job shortly thereafter and spent the rest of the season playing on the kickoff and kickoff return teams (if I was lucky). I remember sitting in the locker room after that game when our trainer—a moonlighting chiropractor—wrapped my arm in gauze and ointment, and tried to convince me that I still had a future in football. He was wrong, but I appreciated the effort.

Our final game of the season was played in McMorran Arena, in Port Huron, Michigan, which is a blue-collar town on the shore of Lake Erie (the unhip Michigan coastline). McMorran was home of the league-leading Port Huron Pirates who, with their high salaries, fake smoke machine, decent-looking cheerleaders, and superior players, were the filet of the CIFL. I dreaded playing there. It was an old-school hockey arena, like the ones portrayed in the movie *Slap Shot*. Port Huron's fans were drunk, loud, and bloodthirsty.

On my way out of the locker room and into the tunnel, I eyed a rolled-up piece of the turf we'd be playing on, and our team doctor, eying me eying the turf, said, "They got this turf from Foxboro Stadium in New England. The Patriots used to play on it."

Needless to say, I was intrigued. From my vantage point on the bench, I spent part of the evening studying the turf. The Foxboro turf always had a certain look—a little flatter, more faded, and less grainy than its AstroTurf counterparts. Simply stated, it looked cheap. By the time it got to the Port Huron Pirates after God knows how many stints in suburban soccer facilities, it was downright threadbare.

* * *

In 1987, I was eleven years old, and each Sunday I worshiped at the First Church of the National Football League. I was enamored with the players, the uniforms, the telecasts, and anything associated with the league. The NFL represented, at the time, the pinnacle of my dreams and the embodiment of everything that was possible in the world. And that embodiment was best captured, melodramatically, by NFL Films, which made an art out of pairing orchestral arrangements with slow-motion highlights. The mid-1980s versions of these films featured experimentations with graphics (cheesy) and the occasional departure from the orchestral classics (also cheesy). But by and large these films served as the backdrop to my dreams.

By 1986, many of the NFL's staid and dynastic franchises, like Pittsburgh and Dallas, had started to crumble, both failing to make the playoffs. Ditto for Miami and Don Shula. It was Dallas's first losing season since 1964. In 1986, Kansas City's special teams unit garnered a bit of fame by blocking nine kicks and scoring several touchdowns. They earned their first playoff berth in fifteen seasons, and their emotional head coach, John Mackovic, wept in the locker room. Three weeks later, he was fired, giving credence to the NFL's unofficial moniker, "Not For Long." By 1986, the sensational quarterback class of 1983 had begun to mature. Jim Kelly was fresh off a three-season sabbatical with the United States Football League's (USFL) Houston Gamblers, who ran the run-and-shoot offense, which allowed Kelly to rack up mad statistical output. Marino threw for 44 touchdowns in 1986 and became the NFL's first quarterback to throw for more than 4,000 yards in 3 different seasons. Marino would become his era's ultimate "great stats, not titles" guy. Other outstanding young quarterbacks included Cincinnati's Boomer Esiason, Cleveland's Bernie Kosar, the New York Jets' Ken O'Brien, and Philadelphia's Randall Cunningham (who, along with other Eagles quarterbacks, was sacked a league-record 104 times). O'Brien threw for 449 yards and 4 touchdowns in the 1986 opener vs. Miami, in a 51–45 victory. He piloted the Jets to victory in ten of their first eleven games before everything came apart, as it often did for the Jets in that era. Kosar passed the once-moribund Browns into the playoffs and engineered a showstopper in double-overtime against the Jets, throwing for 489 yards and propelling the Browns to the American Football Conference (AFC) Championship against John Elway's Broncos. Elway had won more games over the previous three seasons than any other NFL quarterback, and the AFC Championship would provide a setting for "The Drive"—which perhaps, even more than his later Super Bowl victories, would cement the Elway legend.

On a side note, one of the choicest parts of the 1986 NFL Films highlights package is a Giants segment in which Lawrence Taylor is sitting on a sofa in an epic Cosby-style sweater, with two (inexplicable) toddlers sitting on his lap. The piece touted Taylor's "old-fashioned work ethic," of which he was reported to have had very little. What he did have was unbelievably freakish talent and a highly publicized drug problem. Also priceless was this quote about the Giants: "This lunch-pail bunch remained as down-to-earth as the swampland surrounding their stadium." It was accompanied by footage of nose tackle Jim Burt pouring himself a coffee at a local 7-Eleven, which betrayed the NFL's desire to be perceived as just a bunch of workaday Joes like you and me.

San Francisco's Joe Montana would make a heroic return from spinal surgery, only to again be blasted out of the playoffs (and consciousness) on a cold day in the Meadowlands by New York's Jim Burt. The Giants would advance to the Super Bowl and would ultimately win it. The NFL's balance of power was shifting, and labor-relations storm clouds were on the horizon. Montana would play a pivotal role in the unfolding narrative of the 1987 strike.

By the age of eleven, I was able to cognate and reason at a pretty advanced level, yet I still retained the wide-eyed sense of wonder and hero worship that the NFL offered. And then, strangely and (to me) without warning, the NFL Players Association went on strike, setting in motion the oddest and least-talked-about twenty-four-day stretch in NFL history.

At the time I remember the league suspending play for a week, as team owners and players negotiated frantically, wanting to avoid a weeks-long work stoppage like the one that shortened the 1982 season to only nine games. Soon it was decided by ownership that the teams would field "scab" rosters populated by replacement players who would have roughly a week to learn a playbook and get into "game shape." I remember being fascinated by the footage I was seeing—real NFL stars like Lawrence Taylor and Joe Montana marching around with signs in front of their stadiums, while no-names like Sean Payton (then a Chicago replacement quarterback, now a Super Bowl–winning coach) and Marion "Suge" Knight (then of the replacement Los Angeles Rams, now of Death Row Records) put on NFL uniforms and masqueraded, for three weeks, as NFL players in games that actually counted. At eleven, the whole thing seemed to me to be a wonderful lark. My father, who was a standout college and semipro player in the early 1970s, flexed his surgically repaired knees and lamented not being a few years younger.

I knew nothing about labor relations and nothing about what was at stake for the NFL players. I just knew that the guys on these scab rosters were living my dream—they were getting to put on NFL helmets and jerseys each week and getting to play in NFL stadiums.

* * *

It's early 2013, and in my relatively older age (thirty-six) I've continued to dabble in semipro football and have been, for a few years, on a search for odd football experiences. I've collected old USFL DVDs and have found the very first televised game in league history (L.A. Express vs. New Jersey Generals, Herschel Walker's pro debut), a shootout in the Meadowlands between Steve Young (Express) and Doug Flutie (Generals), and a Marcus Dupree game (New Orleans Breakers vs. Chicago Blitz). But the crown jewel in my search for weird football ephemera was tape of the NFL's scab games in 1987. I scoured the Internet and found a few articles, a few photos, but no highlights or footage, and definitely no complete games. There seemed to be a de facto gag order in place as it pertained to the 1987 strike. Clearly it is viewed by the league as a dark, embarrassing stain—something never to be repeated again and, as *Sports Illustrated*'s Peter King called it, "The biggest bastardization in pro football history."

The coaches were stuck in the middle of the player/management dispute. Some, like Philadelphia's Buddy Ryan, sided with players and basically protested the scab games by allegedly doing as little coaching as possible. Some, like Mike Ditka, sided with management, saying famously that "these [scabs] are the *real* Chicago Bears."[1] Most though, like Cleveland's Marty Schottenheimer, just said, "We can't feel sorry for ourselves. I'm a football coach, and I'll coach whoever is here."[2]

Replacement rosters included surrealities, like thirty-seven-year-old former USFL quarterback John Reaves and Tony Robinson, a Washington Redskins quarterback out on a prison work-release program, cultural curiosities like small-college running back Joe Dudek who once graced a *Sports Illustrated* cover alongside Bo Jackson, and strike breakers like New York Jets defensive end Mark Gastineau, who never regained the respect of his teammates and Lawrence Taylor, who never lost the respect of his.

In January 2013, I submitted the kind of football book upon which writers like myself make a living. It was a gentle analysis of rookie sensation Robert Griffin III's first season as a Washington Redskin, which will, I hope, sell a lot of copies and lead to more opportunities like it. I also ghostwrote a book with former NFL quarterback Jim Kelly for a different publisher, and while these projects paid bills, they kept me, momentarily, from my search for 1987 scab game stories, until I found a probably disreputable dealer on the Internet selling bootlegged DVDs of NFL games spanning all eras. Each of the discs were ten dollars even, and viewers could choose from a smorgasbord that included past Super Bowls, classic playoff matchups, and meaningless preseason games. I quickly signed up for a "membership" to the site and then nervously entered my payment information, rendering payment for one of the four scab games this collector had for sale.

The game is an October 4 clash between the scab Browns and the scab Patriots in Foxboro (then Sullivan) Stadium, on the selfsame turf on which I'd played at McMorran Arena. This, I thought, was notable, and it became the deciding factor as I chose this game and not one of the others.

One week later, I eagerly ripped into the hand-lettered envelope and popped the disc it contained into my DVD player.

By the middle of the first quarter, I'd viewed

- Footage of the New England picket line, featuring quarterback Tony Eason, unshaven in a hoodie, looking sad, cold, and ordinary, and one of the Patriot offensive linemen signing autographs for fans while wearing his helmet. Thus begins a long list of "things you would never see in today's image-conscious NFL."
- Three fumbles by starting halfback Tony Collins, who had, at the time, already scored thirty-one touchdowns in his career. Either it was an unfathomably bad game by the veteran or he bet on Cleveland.
- Two bad punt snaps by Cleveland replacement long snapper, Mike Katolin, whose only NFL experience was the three strike games in 1987, though he had a nice career in the USFL. I felt for him, as in the fraternity of long snappers you never want to see a

brother fail, unless, perhaps, he's competing with you for the same job. Actually, not even then.

- Cleveland quarterback Jeff Christensen, shown squeegeeing water off the turf during pregame warm-ups (see also, things that would never happen today). Christensen looked so forlorn, pushing the small device over the fake green turf—an exercise which, it was obvious to all, made absolutely no difference in the turf's quality or traction.
- Two fumbles by New England quarterback Bob Bleier, cousin of Pittsburgh Steelers legend Rocky Bleier.
- Keith Bosley, starting at offensive tackle for the Browns, who was reported to weigh 320 pounds but looked as though he tipped the scales around 420. "He wears size 5X shoulder pads!" said announcer Don Criqui, who was clearly at a loss for things to talk about.
- The Patriots offense rack up a total of three yards and the Browns, prolific by comparison, rack up fifteen.

It was horrible pro football, and weirdly, in spite of the ineptitude I was viewing, I was hooked. Hooked, because this is clearly the most bizarre piece of NFL history I'd encountered, and it made me hungry for the story behind the story of the NFL strike games. The games have been referred to in the film *The Replacements*, a poorly written, slapstick vehicle for Keanu Reeves, but to my knowledge have never been deeply explored in print. This book is part curiosity and part ascetic exercise, because I know that these games may be painful to watch. Still, I feel that there is a debt owed to all of the players on both sides of the dispute to tell their stories and to shine some light on a shrouded period of NFL history.

This book will be a journey into the darkest and most secretive three weeks in NFL history and a look inside the games you can't buy and the footage you can't find. It will tell the stories of the men who were Bears, Browns, and Patriots in uniform only. It will explore the experiences of real NFL veterans and cultural oddities living a dream, like long snapper Joe Bock and wide receiver Larry Linne. It will contrast the innocence and joy experienced by the scabs with the high-stakes negotiations being waged by striking NFL players—negotiations that would eventually spike the pay scale and change the face of the NFL forever.

I

PLANES, TRAINS, AND AUTOMOBILES

The Football Nomad: Mike Hohensee

The replacement Chicago Bears arrived in Philadelphia's Veterans Stadium on October 4 at 2:07 a.m., under the cover of night. Coaches and staff slept in penthouse skyboxes atop the stadium. Clubhouse boys slept with the equipment to make sure it wouldn't be stolen, and players stretched out in the locker room to grab whatever sleep was possible. At 6:32 a.m., the replacement Eagles were bussed past the picket line and into Veterans Stadium.

Chicago Bears head coach Mike Ditka chomped on a large cigar. It was business as usual. "Coach Ditka's philosophy was that he coached who was in the room," remembers Bears replacement quarterback Mike Hohensee. "He addressed us calmly and professionally, and he coached us hard."

Hohensee was already something of a football nomad by 1987, having played for the USFL's Washington Federals, as well as logging time in the Canadian Football League (CFL) and Arena Football League after a standout college career for a struggling program at the University of Minnesota. In fact, his signing with Chicago made him the first football player to suit up in each professional league.

"I was tending bar and sharing an apartment when I got the call," he remembers. "There was a message for me to call somebody from the Chicago Bears. I ignored it because I thought it was my roommate trying to play a joke on me. But then he said, 'Hey, did you call the Bears back?' and I knew it was legit."

Being that it was the pre–cell phone, pre-text, pre-email, and pre–social media era, NFL scouts and coaches scrambled to evaluate and connect with potential replacement players, often pulling them out of day jobs midstream. Hohensee had recently wrapped up a season in the Arena League and was still relatively sharp and relatively fit.

"I was worried," he recalls, "because I had been lifting and running, but I hadn't been throwing a lot. I was normally a workout freak, but there just wasn't much time to get ready."

Hohensee initially saw the call from Chicago as an unqualified "great opportunity." But the magnitude of the labor dispute behind it dawned on him as he followed news reports and the game drew near. Still, he said, the Bears made sure that replacement players were shielded from the drama, didn't have to cross picket lines, and were well prepared. "A lot of us came from the Arena League," he recalls, "so we were used to playing in games and contributing to teams. I think that gave the Bears an advantage."

A picketing Philadelphia Eagle wore a t-shirt emblazoned with "Scabs Come from Cuts." A strong union town, the picket line was bolstered by locals in nylon Teamsters jackets shouting "No scabs!" There was a strange sense of solidarity between young, relatively wealthy professional athletes and the workaday Joes who shelled out to watch them perform.

Perhaps labor is always labor and management is always management, regardless of the size of the numbers involved. However, one negative manifestation of the huge player salaries today is that players and fans seem to exist on different planets. By and large they eat at different restaurants, drink at different bars, and take different vacations. The pro-athlete financial needle has moved from "well compensated" to "freakishly rich" for most players, making them conceptually and practically unavailable to most fans.

In Philadelphia, AFL-CIO union supporters stood shoulder to shoulder with Pro Bowlers. Curious fans had to push their way through a hostile picket line. Several fans were shoved to the ground in their attempt to get to the turnstiles.

Veterans Stadium was nearly empty on the cool, clear Sunday afternoon of October 4 as 41,000 season tickets were returned to the Eagles ticket office. The upper-level seats, yellow and red, seemed completely deserted, as one of the league's most loyal and passionate fan bases stayed away en masse. A set of field-level portable bleachers—spanning the length of the field—was simply covered by a giant black tarp. Nevertheless, the game would count toward league standings. No striking Bears or Eagles had yet crossed the line, meaning that an NFL regular season game would be played entirely by replacements. The Eagles "boasted" six players who had, at one time, had experience in the league; the Bears only two.

In Chicago there was a history of divisiveness between players and ownership. Bears owner Mike McCaskey—grandson of the late George Halas—was seen as snobby and elitist. A graduate of Yale (where, to be fair, he did play football) he was wingtips and sport coats and country clubs amidst a team that saw itself as blue collar and tough. He didn't fit in, was perceived as cheap, and was openly mocked by many of his players.[1] Said Jim McMahon in Steve Delsohn's book, *Da Bears*, "McCaskey had no clue."[2]

By 1987, the mystique of the dominant 1985 club was well on its way to wearing off. Buddy Ryan was long gone (departing right after the Super Bowl victory over New England), McMahon was injured more often than he was healthy and openly feuded with his owner, and the club was grooming Neal Anderson to take over the running game from the aging Walter Payton. Indeed, Chicago seemed to be a study in human nature run wild, as egos clashed and players and coaches openly resented one another for the amount of "off-field" endorsements and opportunities they were garnering. What could have been a great NFL dynasty instead became a case study in how not to handle success.

The strike's free agency battleground had practical implications for the Bears as well. Viewed as one of the league's cheapest franchises, the Bears would routinely bus to a local high school field for practice and lacked an indoor facility in spite of the city's notoriously brutal winters. They would often travel to Champaign to use the University of Illinois indoor bubble or even practice in random Southern cities during the weeks leading up to playoff games. There was the feeling that before free agency and player movement, the Bears didn't need to "compete" with the rest of the league when it came to facilities. Said tight end Tim Wrightman in *Da Bears*, "When I first went to the Bears I said 'This is the NFL?' The locker rooms and the facilities at UCLA were ten times better."[3]

"We practiced all over the place," said tight end Emery Moorehead in the same book. "Then we would bus back to Lake Forest at rush hour on the Eisenhower Expressway in full uniform like a high school team."[4]

A group of unknowns loosened up on the threadbare Veterans Stadium AstroTurf, known for being among the worst in the league. Being that it was the pre-stadium-naming-rights era (by and large), municipalities still ran many of the league's stadiums, and many late 1980s NFL cities still had "multiuse" stadiums wherein the local NFL team shared carpet and facilities with the local Major League Baseball (MLB) club. At one time seen as marvels of modern engineering, by 1987, many of these cookie-cutter stadiums—like the ones in Pittsburgh, Cincinnati, and Philadelphia—were viewed as gauche, charmless, and inferior. And near the end of the season in those cities, when the carpet inevitably froze, players had the sensation of playing on near concrete, and watching those games took on a new level of painfulness.

"AstroTurf was introduced in response to very poor quality natural grass athletic fields," explains Dr. Ron Calhoun, who served for seventeen years as a turf grass extension specialist at Michigan State University. "For years, natural turf fields were grown on native soil root zones. Native soil fields often have too much silt and clay (small soil particles). These soils present a lot of problems in that they tend to stay dry when they are dry and stay wet when they are wet. In addition, they will typically become overly compacted and cause a situation where the turf struggles, thins out, and dies. AstroTurf was supposed to address the shortcomings of natural grass fields, and reduce maintenance costs, and increase revenue by allowing for unlimited field use, and last a really long time.

"The original AstroTurf field design was pretty simple. Essentially, indoor/outdoor carpeting over a really dense foam all glued to asphalt. The fields were sold with the promise of lasting for thirty-plus years. As you know, most of this turned out to be campaign promises. One of the major problems with the early fields was that the dense foam substrate disintegrated and needed to be replaced. I'm pretty sure none of the carpets lasted thirty years either. One Big Ten school replaced the substrate three times in fifteen years."

Today I'm almost nostalgic for those buildings; for the concrete, the lack of polish, the lack of gigantic high-definition (HD) replay screens, the carpet. However, having played on it, I will say that AstroTurf had to be one of the worst and most sadistic inventions in the history of athletics. Any football player who played any amount of time on turf simply maintained a collection of oozing, open burns on his skin for the duration of the season. The only universe in which this was a good idea was one dominated by television aesthetics (no mud, no grass stains) and the bottom line.

I remember scaling what felt like a straight-up staircase in Cincinnati's Riverfront Stadium as a child, feeling exhilarated but also like I was a mile away from the action taking place on the carpet. The last of the large, concrete multiuse buildings is home to the CFL's Toronto Argonauts and MLB's Blue Jays, and will soon, no doubt, be replaced by something more posh, more comfortable, and more corporate.

A Bears returner named Lorenzo Lynch returns the opening kickoff of replacement football to almost the fifty-yard line. Incidentally, Lynch was one of a few replacements who made such an impression that he was kept around after the strike.[5] The Eagles' replacement kicker, Dave Jacobs, is injured on the play—one in which broadcaster Terry Bradshaw refers to Lynch as (mysteriously) "Jacobs" several times. Bradshaw went on to opine that Jacobs will be replaced by Eagles utility player Guido Merkens, who had NFL experience as a quarterback, running back, receiver, and defensive back.

Hohensee's first NFL play is a toss to running back Anthony Mosley for no gain. Ditka seems content to pound the ball on the ground with Mosley and Lakei Heimuli, a native of Tonga who made the final cut with the Bears and was the only draft choice to return during the replacement games. Hohensee's first pass is over the head of Glen Kozlowski.

For his part, Mike Ditka's public posture was, at this point in the strike, almost entirely positive toward his replacements. He spoke of the fun the players were having and the enthusiasm they brought to the game. "This is part of the American Dream," he explained. "They're just trying to grasp one last straw . . . that's all they want out of life. They're not bad kids, believe me." The time period is vintage Ditka—what with the ever-present "Bears" sweater, this time covered by a black sport coat, paired with sunglasses and a golf cap. Today's NFL suffers from a distinct sartorial and personality deficiency at the head coach position.

Hohensee remembers Ditka, always a showman with a big personality, for his technical football acumen. "He could walk into any position group meeting on the team and run it," he recalls. "Ditka had an incredible knowledge of the game . . . and because of his big personality, often doesn't get credit for it."

A week into the strike, Ditka was enamored enough with Hohensee to suggest that he could stick around, despite the presence of Jim Harbaugh, Mike Tomczak, and Doug Flutie on the roster [6] Whether he was being authentic or whether this was just a way to leverage his regulars back into the fold, is hard to say.

"He coached me hard," Hohensee says. "There was one time that he really tore into me on the practice field, but he didn't let me leave without building me back up again first."

Lining up in the shotgun formation, Hohensee and the Bears go for it on fourth down, but the pass falls incomplete, meaning that he will have to wait a little longer for his first NFL completion. The pass is deflected by former San Diego Chargers draft choice Fred Smalls. The 5,000 fans in attendance roar their approval.

The first big hit of the game came courtesy of Chicago linebacker Jay Norvell, who played collegiately at Iowa and in 2015 is now a wide receiver's coach at the University of Texas. Norvell's coaching resume is emblematic of the nomadic life of a football coach—with stops at Iowa, Northern Iowa, Wisconsin, Iowa State, Nebraska, and UCLA, in addition to stints with the Colts and the Raiders.[7] Chicago's linebacking corps also featured a player named Bobby Bell, whose father was a Hall of Fame linebacker for the Kansas City Chiefs in the 1960s.

Chicago, by the way, did an admirable job of keeping its replacement players out of the jersey numbers of regular players. As a result, almost every linebacker wore a number in the nineties, which creates an odd visual aesthetic.

Keeping replacements out of regular numbers was especially difficult in Chicago, with a bevy of actual retired numbers, de facto retired numbers, and legendary players still under contract like Walter Payton and Mike Singletary.

Chicago seems content to run toss sweeps behind John Wojciechowski and Jack Oliver. They utilize motion and run out of multiple formations but still ran primarily to the left. Hohensee's first completion is to a tight end named Don Kindt, whose father was a first-round draft choice of the Chicago Bears in 1947. The younger Kindt had been in training camps with the Bears and the Green Bay Packers, a testament to the fact that contrary to popular belief, most of these replacements were good football players with at least some pro experience.

Rumor had it that Buddy Ryan—so disgusted by the owners' decision to use replacement players—would protest the game by refusing to coach or by doing very little coaching. But early on at least he appeared active and involved, wearing a headset and blitzing his defenders often. The Ryan/Ditka feud was, by 1987, deeply ingrained and highly publicized. The two had to be separated in the halftime locker room by their respective units in 1985, when Buddy Ryan's fame as a defensive coordinator threatened to overtake that of Ditka. Ryan's defensive players, fiercely loyal, carried him off the field after Chicago's victory in Super Bowl XX. It was clear at that point that the two megapersonalities would not coexist on one staff. Ryan would routinely take credit when the Bears won and blame the offense when they lost, and he also broke one of the longest-running unwritten clubhouse rules in sports when he would routinely air his dirty laundry toward players and coaching colleagues via the media. Theirs was one of the most openly toxic and, thereby, entertaining coach/assistant coach feuds in all of professional sports. Not surprisingly, Ryan was also involved in perhaps the second most toxic coach-on-coach relationship in pro football when he assaulted Houston Oilers offensive coordinator Kevin Gilbride on the sideline during a game.

When Ryan arrived in Philadelphia, he famously declared, "There's a winner in town."[8] When Ryan was introduced at a press conference as the Eagles' new head coach, beaming owner Norman Braman referred to him as "the next Vince Lombardi of the National Football League."[9]

Ditka responded the next day by saying, "Never again in history will an assistant get as much credit as Buddy did."[10] Ryan did, however, change the shape of both offensive and defensive football for years to come. Because his Chicago defenses were so talentless in the late 1970s, Ryan authored exotic blitz packages that would overload the line of scrimmage and, in particular, overload certain sides of the ball. The philosophy finally reached its apex in 1985 when he had the players—including Mike Singletary, Otis Wilson, Wilber Marshall, Richard Dent, et al.—to run it to perfection. This ultraaggressive scheme forced offensive masterminds like Bill Walsh and the architects of the run-and-shoot to spread the field and send multiple receivers on short, high-percentage routes. This eventually took the teeth out of Ryan's vaunted "46" defense.

The regular Eagles were led by one of the league's most sensational young talents—a running quarterback named Randall Cunningham, who, in 1987, was still a year away from a string of Pro Bowl appearances that had him on the cusp of superstardom. At one time it was thought that the charismatic Cunningham would become the Michael Jordan of pro football, both from a playing and marketing perspective. It wasn't to be, however, as "Buddyball" proved limited.[11]

Ryan's replacements, however, struggle to stop Hohensee and his collection of receivers, as Hohensee connects with Lakei Heimuli for a score halfway through the first quarter.

"I'm out on strike because of all the guys who save me every Sunday," says Eagles Pro Bowl receiver Mike Quick from outside the stadium. "We're fighting for better benefits for guys who will play this game after we're gone. The local unions came down and they're doing a great job showing that they appreciate the real Eagles."

Inside, the replacement Eagles continued to take a beating. Quarterback Scott Tinsley, formerly of the University of Southern California (USC), has already taken a beating by the end of the first quarter, enduring a number of sacks and quarterback hurries, including a safety blitz by Chicago's Egypt Allen.[12] As a result, the Eagles mostly feed carries to running back Reggie Brown, who was with the Atlanta Falcons in 1982, the USFL's Los Angeles Express in 1983–1984, and Arizona Outlaws in 1985. Tinsley's most successful plays are screens to Brown, one of the only ways to neutralize Chicago's aggressive, blitzing defense, which is a facsimile of Ryan's famous "46" defense, but instead of Otis Wilson and Wilber Marshall flying off the edge, it is Norvell and Bell.[13]

Philadelphia's most significant drive of the half is marked by a Tinsley pass to Mike Siano, a Philadelphia rugby player. A delay-of-game call on Tinsley, and a downfield pass that is almost intercepted by Bear Steve Trimble, combine to stall the drive. Trimble is wearing number 40, most famously worn in Chicago by running back Gale Sayers.

Chicago is notoriously lethargic when it comes to appropriate and timely jersey retirements for legendary players like Sayers and Dick Butkus (and for that matter, Ditka). Seeing Trimble wearing Sayers's number 40 would be akin to a replacement Boston Celtic wearing Larry Bird's "33." For the record, it was also weird seeing linebacker Jim Morrissey wearing number 51 and a variety of Bears wearing "89."

The telecast takes an absurd turn in the second quarter, when Irv Cross interviews a fan seated on the first row who explains that he is a roommate of Eagles replacement linebacker Chuck Gorecki, and that Gorecki had in fact been getting harassing/threatening phone calls and that he came to the stadium to support his friend and roommate because "football is one of the hardest games to play." You can tell that Cross (a former player himself) feels super weird about doing this sort of interview, but you can also, almost, hear the director in his earpiece making him do it.[14]

What's strange about this game is how *not-bad* it is, given that these guys really only had a week together. There has only been one turnover and very few penalties. The Philly crowd rumbles to life only when Guido Merkens enters the game at quarterback in the second quarter, perhaps signaling the end of the Scott Tinsley era after a quarter and a half.

"He'll run it," explains Terry Bradshaw. When asked how he knew Merkens would run, he replies, simply, "Guido Merkens is a total athlete."

Merkens is sacked for a six-yard loss.

* * *

A Bears drive in the second quarter features an eighteen-yard scramble by Hohensee, followed by a deep crossing route to wide receiver Ken Knapczyk, who played his college ball at Northern Iowa and was working in a mill in Mokena, Illinois, before the strike.[15]

CUT TO: Irv Cross again, with his microphone, ever the roving, intrepid reporter, this time reporting live from the press box where he is surrounded by all manner of balding, grizzled, note-taking 1980s-style Philadelphia sports reporters, one of whom he interviews about the quality of the football and who, not surprisingly, responds by saying something dour about the lack of quality on the field. (Incidentally, if you're wondering why I'm devoting so much time to Cross's interviews in specific and the absurdity of this whole thing in general, it's because I find the up-front nature of the absurdity so refreshing and entertaining, whereas today's absurdity is sort of hidden behind sixty-six HD camera angles and lots of in-game effects. This absurdity is just sort of out there, which is what makes it so great. Either way, Cross deserved a very substantial drink at the completion of this game, and I'm sure he got one courtesy of one of these very grizzled, Scotch-guzzling media members.) This is something we rarely see in the modern era, being that "reporters" are now electronically tethered to social media to the degree that an NFL press box looks like a college-town coffee shop, what with everybody buried in his or her smartphone or laptop.

Hohensee ends the drive on a beautiful blitz-pickup and fade route to Glen Kozlowski for a touchdown, which resulted in the quote of the day from Terry Bradshaw, who reflects, "I never played with one Polish wide receiver . . . the Bears have two, in Knapczyk and Kozlowski. A lot of Polish pride on the field today."

CUT TO: Cross with Eagles owner Norman Braman who says of the strike, "It's a tragedy for the fans . . . you look at the hooliganism that occurred outside our stadium . . . it's a tragedy for the city of Philadelphia . . . everything our founding fathers tried to accomplish, you saw the opposite out there today. The only thing missing was the Ku Klux Klan.[16] I think what Gene Upshaw did was take the lid off that bottle and order for all the ghouls and the devils to come out. What you saw here is something that brought out the worst elements in this city. It's a disgrace to the city of Philadelphia and should be an embarrassment to everyone who's watching here today."

Cross deftly comments on how it appears that the picketing moved away from even being about the players and turned into something else entirely. He then allows an emotional Braman to continue in the vein of the above.

The more I watch these Cross cutaways, the more I think there's actually a crude kind of genius to his body of work on October 4, 1987. It was raw, and the opposite of overproduced, making it, in a strange way, a precursor to the reality television that is all the rage now.[17]

"Irv, we asked the players not to strike," Braman says. "We asked them to have federal mediators in, and they refused. That request was made a dozen times. I just think it's a tragedy and especially a tragedy for the fans."

CBS cuts to a section of empty seats, populated by a few fans who hold a banner simply reading, "This is Sad."

It occurs to me as the cameras cut back to the action that what the viewer is seeing is the best kind of satire and commentary, and it is pulled off with the barest of bare minimum effects, gadgetry, and so forth. The CBS telecast of October 4, 1987, manages to be beautiful and poignant without a ton of cameras, sideline reporters, graphics, and music. There is a real "less is more" quality to the production.

* * *

A Philadelphia lineman, Paul Ryczek, works as a stockbroker in Atlanta. He expresses elation over the fact that his last name was spelled correctly on his jersey. He explains that as a stockbroker he spends so much time cold-calling and dealing with rejection, that he was afraid to call teams and face rejection once again. Another Eagles tight end, Jay Repko, owns a banquet catering business. The Eagles also field a defensive tackle named Gary Bolden out of Southwest Oklahoma State, who learned of the strike when he was wrestling professionally under the moniker "Stagger Lee." Needing to get out of his wrestling commitment at once, he staged a fake broken leg and was carried out of the venue on a stretcher so that he could hop a plane and become a Philadelphia Eagle.

Buddy Ryan called Bolden "the funnest [sic] human being I've ever been with." Bolden was also known as "The Kickin' Mule," but after a sixty-pound weight gain, apparently grew out of a kicking opportunity and into a spot on the defensive line.

One of the aspects of the game that suffered the most during strike football was special teams. In one of the games, total athlete Guido Merkens, also the Eagles replacement punter, fields a low snap and is engulfed by Chicago defenders, giving Hohensee another opportunity to score just before the half. On his first play from scrimmage he runs a play action boot pass and finds his fullback, Al Wolden, out of Bemidji State (MN), running free on a wheel route up the right sideline. Wolden was another training camp player for the Bears in 1987, as many of the replacement players signed agreements after they were cut in camp, indicating that they would come back in the event of a strike.[18] The play is initially ruled a score, but sadly, Wolden's moment in the sun is negated by a replay reversal. This seems especially nefarious in a replacement game but is a subtle reminder that the games do count. On the following play, Wolden leads his tailback, Chris Brewer, into the end zone on a simple isolation play. Future Super Bowl–winning head coach Sean Payton holds for the extra point. The adjective "boyish" doesn't begin to describe Payton. He looks almost prepubescent, even in his Bears uniform.

Today, Wolden teaches physical education at a middle school in Red Lake, Minnesota—the name of which evokes images of leaves falling and fishing trips and snowmobiling in the winter. Red Lake, he reminds me, was home to an unspeakably sad school shooting in 2005 that took the lives of five students as well as one of Wolden's teaching colleagues. He admits that "going back to work each day, where it happened, is difficult." Wolden's comments are a reminder that in addition to excelling at athletics, these young men all have personal stories that often end up much richer. Wolden explains in his perfectly friendly sounding upper-Midwest accent, that his chief joy these days comes from being a husband and a father to two small boys.

His wife posted a YouTube video of his football highlights that is nine minutes in length—spanning two AC/DC songs. There's something of such deep love and devotion in the act of doing this—a wife making a tribute video for her husband's long-past college football career—that makes me smile. The video shows a big, smooth, athletic, and physical small-college running back who is just a little bit more talented than his competition. Bears camp, for Wolden, revealed that although he felt comfortable at the pro level, the athleticism was another matter entirely.

"Walter Payton was in his last camp in 1987, and there were some rumblings that maybe he was losing a step or two," Wolden recalls. "After one play where he made a great cut and broke a couple of tackles, he came back to where I was standing, put his arm around me and asked, 'Al, have I still got it?' I said, 'Yeah, you've still got it.' Payton was like a little kid. He was always smiling and had so much energy. One time during a rookie camp practice, we were with our backfield coach Johnny Roland when we heard a loud bang, like somebody detonated some dynamite. Johnny just shook his head and said, 'That's Walter.'

"I could see the writing on the wall after I made it through a couple of cuts but wasn't getting the reps in practice," he explains. "Coach Ditka brought me in and said 'Al, you do everything pretty average . . . but on this level you have to do at least one thing great.'"

"I heard a rumor about the strike on the news," Wolden remembers. "And then I got a call from Ken Geiger, who was an awesome guy and a liaison from the Bears who asked me if I wanted to come in. I said, 'I need a little time to think about it,' and he replied, 'I'll call you back in ten minutes.'

"After I hung up, I called my father, who was a longtime labor union guy on the railroad and a member of the United Steelworkers union. I needed his blessing before I could move forward. I said, 'Dad there's gonna be a strike.' He said, 'Go for it. None of those guys [regular players] are going to go hungry.'"

The next day, Wolden was in his apartment when the phone rang. A FedEx truck idled outside his apartment at Bemidji State, where he was finishing up some coursework for his degree. The FedEx guy delivered a contract and a plane ticket for a flight from Bemidji to Chicago where the Bears would have only a few days to prepare for Philadelphia.

"It was what I wanted to do since I was a little kid," he explains. "To play in a real game, on national television. It was exciting. When they announced the strike was over, I was sad, honestly. I was making 4,000 bucks a week playing football and living a dream."

※ ※ ※

The telecast is pure reality television, as the network cuts again to striking star Mike Quick, who is given a chance to respond to Braman's inflammatory press box comments. Quick explains that Philadelphia is "a union town" and that union members simply came out in support of the "real Eagles." He adds that the striking Eagles have "no control" over how nonplayers do or don't behave on the picket line. He is wearing aviator sunglasses, a Cosby sweater, and an NFLPA ball cap.

The Philadelphia kicking game, ever an adventure, surrenders another score as a Guido Merkens punt is blocked and returned for a Bear touchdown to stretch the lead to 28–3.[19] Given one more opportunity just before halftime, Hohensee pilots a surprisingly effective two-minute drill, finding Kozlowski with several passes and maneuvering the Bears deep into the red zone. Hohensee caps the half with another touchdown pass off of play action on the goal line, hitting tight end Don Kindt in the back corner of the end zone. It is his third scoring strike of the game.

✿ ✿ ✿

Perhaps the worst game of the first week of the strike involves the two teams—the Saints and Rams—who have the greatest percentage of players who have already crossed the picket line. In the nearly empty Pontiac Silverdome (Detroit is another fiercely union area) former Arizona State star Todd Hons led the Lions in a shootout with the Mike Hold–led Tampa Bay Bucs.

Strike breaker Gary Hogeboom passed a strong Colts team to a lopsided victory over the Bills, throwing five touchdown passes.

There were bad snaps and blocked kicks all over the league, given that snappers, holders, and kickers rely so much on timing and rapport to perfect their craft. Indeed, football as a whole is a game that operates on a certain high, unspoken level of trust and camaraderie, so it's strange to see football being played with no semblance of either.

CUT TO: Irv Cross in a stadium tunnel with former Bears linebacking legend Dick Butkus, who explains that "there's always a '51' on the field," in reference to the fact that his old number has been issued to replacement Bear Mark Rodenhauser. He says that it's "not a big deal to me," and then goes on to explain exactly why it's a big deal. The thing is, it *is* a big deal. As fan of the Bears and as a fan of linebacking in general, Butkus can do no wrong in my opinion. Noncommittal on the strike itself, he says, "I'm here to do a game for the people [in radio] I work for."

✿ ✿ ✿

Sean Payton starts the second half for the Bears, fresh off a stint in the Arena League where he played for the Chicago Bruisers then joined CFL's Ottawa Rough Riders. When Payton left college at Eastern Illinois, he did so as the third leading passer in college football history (yardage).

Hohensee remembers long nights spent studying the playbook with Payton, which foretold his future as an offensive innovator. "I just remember that he wanted to get the offense down, and he wanted to get it right," says Hohensee. Payton improvises after a low shotgun snap on his first series, and scrambles for twenty-eight yards before being inexplicably benched in favor of Hohensee, who throws an interception to safety Mike Kullman, who played three seasons of semipro ball before playing collegiately at Kutztown State.

Guido Merkens leads the replacement Eagles onto the field in their attempt to make the game respectable. At that time it is discovered that, in fact, his last name (Merkens) is misspelled on his jersey (Merkins). It seems fitting somehow. The third quarter feels interminable. At some point during a long Chicago drive, analyst Terry Bradshaw reveals, between guffaws, that "Mark Twain is my favorite poet."[20] I find myself longing for another Irv Cross cutaway. Paid attendance is announced at 4,074.

Regular Eagles tight end John Spagnola is shown signing autographs and then wandering away from the picket line, his job finished for the day. Replacement Eagle tight end Ron Fazio was recently in the employ of a Fitness and Racquet Club owned by regular Eagles Spagnola and Mike Quick. Regarding Spagnola, it's difficult to feel too sorry for a professional athlete who owns a share of a racquet club. These are, as they say, "first-world problems."

During the third quarter, CBS cuts to a bizarre clip of a fan being punched directly in the mouth by what we can assume is a picketing teamster. The fan—mustachioed and wearing a flannel shirt—is stunned for a moment but doesn't go down, while the other guy assumes a fighter's crouch with his hands up. The clip is jarring in its violence, which is ironic given that we're watching actual violence taking place every play on the field. It's bizarre, I think, in that it's happening (for one), but more bizarre in that the NFL is allowing it to air, which can be added to the list of things one would never see in today's slickly packaged and image-freakish NFL.

Mike Hohensee gives way to Payton for good midway through the third quarter. His wildly successful three-touchdown afternoon is in direct contrast to that of Guido Merkens, who has been sacked, hurried, forced to fumble, had a punt blocked, and had his jersey and helmet ripped off multiple times by Chicago defenders. He is sacked ten times for sixty-two yards. It may be, informally, the worst day ever experienced by an NFL quarterback/utility player. He looks miserable and finishes the day broken, on his back, on the Veterans Stadium turf.

Bradshaw and Irv Cross end the telecast on a serious note, essentially saying "no more of this."

Hohensee's strike experience is markedly different. He throws for over 300 yards and 4 touchdowns against 1 pick. There is serious talk of Hohensee being signed to the regular Bear roster until he is injured in the third week of strike action. After the strike is resolved, he is released without fanfare. On his way out of the Bear offices, just before getting into his car and driving away from the NFL forever, he is stopped by the high-pitched voice of Bear legend Walter Payton, in his last NFL season.

"Hey, Hohensee!" Payton shouts. "You did a good job."

2

DIDN'T WE ALMOST HAVE IT ALL

The Meat and Seafood Guy: Joe Bock

The last time I saw Joe Bock we were both under contract with the fledgling Continental Indoor Football League, and we were both sort of publicity stunts—me for my ESPN.com column and Joe because he was in his mid-forties at the time and was a former NFL player.[1] He had already made "history" that season by becoming the first traded player in CIFL/GLIFL (Great Lakes Indoor Football League)[2] history, being dealt from his hometown Rochester Raiders to the struggling (read: winless) New York/New Jersey Revolution, who were unique in that they had no home arena and every game they played was a road game. Simply put, the Revolution were getting slaughtered every week, and I saw it as my opportunity to log significant playing time, given that I had already lost my job as starting long snapper and was being kept around only because of the column and book deal.

I'm not sure Bock even saw the field that evening, in front of what couldn't have been more than 600 people in Battle Creek's Kellogg Arena, in spite of the fact that even at age forty-six he was probably the best player on his team. Still, afterward he was good natured and posed for a photo with me, as I was probably one of the few people in the building who knew and appreciated him from his time with the Houston Gamblers—where he played with future Pro Football Hall of Famer Jim Kelly—and the Birmingham Stallions—where he played with future NFL stars like Joe Cribbs and Cliff Stoudt—both part of the

United States Football League (USFL).[3] We were both genuinely happy to be there even though our seasons hadn't gone as planned.

We were both there because football is an addiction. It's a compulsive behavior. That's the only way to explain why a forty-six-year-old man would risk, at some level, life and limb, in order to play indoor football on threadbare turf in front of 600 mostly disinterested mid-Michiganders. People romantically call it "the love of the game," but I call it an addiction that can be at best a mystery to friends and family and at worst the thing that destroys your relationships with said friends and family in much the same way that a drug addiction does. You do it not even because it's "fun," but because you somehow need to be able to say that you do it.

Bock, in fact, made it into the CIFL/GLIFL on his own merit, at age forty-six.

"I was forty-six years old and my second wife had just filed for divorce," he explains. "I read this thing in the paper about the Rochester Raiders signing forty-three-year-old quarterback Mark Rypien, and thought to myself, 'I can still play at forty-six.' I trained all of January and February and worked out with all of my PE classes . . . I would run with one class, lift with another class, and play games with another. I could still dunk a basketball. Anyway, I went through 8 weeks of training camp, during which the team brought 250 guys in for looks. On the very last play of practice, I was blocking in a one-on-one pass rush drill and dislocated my pinkie finger. I popped it back into place and then a couple of plays later, same thing. It was sticking out at a ninety-degree angle. I told the coach I'd better have a doctor look at it.

"I sat at the hospital for three hours in absolute agony . . . along with my seven-year-old son, who was with me on a school night. Finally, just after they gave me a shot to numb the excruciating pain, the general manager called to tell me I'd made the team."

Bock had made the club as a backup center, starting long snapper, and backup defensive end/nose tackle. After the second game of the season, in which he sprained his knee, he was placed on the inactive list. That's when Bock decided to broker his own trade to the New York/New Jersey Revolution. "I put on a shirt and tie and went all the way to Port Huron to ask their coach if he'd take me for the rest of the year. He said, 'We only pay the league minimum,' and I said 'I paid 500 bucks just to get here to ask you this. I'm not in it for the money.'"

In the first iteration of his football life, Bock played a total of three USFL seasons, two NFL regular season games during the 1987 strike season, one game in the Arena Football League in 1988, and then a smattering of games with two teams in the low-rent CIFL. It is, to me, a meandering and fascinating football resume, and I have the utmost respect for it.

"Isn't there some kind of tipping point where it's better to have not played in the NFL than to have tasted it for two replacement games during the strike season?" my wife asks, as I tell her about Bock.

I look at her like she's crazy. I would have given a limb to be able to suit up twice (for two different teams—Bills and Cardinals—but I'll get to that) during the strike season. The fact that Bock is somewhat tormented by his football circumstance just makes it that much more literary and romantic.

Today Bock is a gym teacher who rotates between two inner-city elementary schools in Rochester, New York. His kids, by and large, don't know that he was a star at Virginia and later a pro football player. "I low-key that aspect of my life," he explains, though it becomes clear pretty quickly that he spends a great deal of time thinking about that aspect of his life in much the same way as we all perseverate over aspects of our life that could have gone (so to speak) "either way."

Before the elementary schools, Bock was a gym teacher/in-school-suspension guy in the toughest inner-city high school in Rochester. It was the kind of place where he was routinely breaking up fights and confiscating guns and drugs. "I was part cop, part coach, part counselor, and part father to these kids," he explains. He also explains that every day at football practice he would scrimmage with the players without pads on, flying around the field, blocking and tackling without the benefit of a helmet or shoulder pads. "You should know that you're talking to a crazy person here," he says. Duly noted.

After a distinguished USFL career with Houston and Birmingham, he was unceremoniously cut loose just like every other USFL player after that league "won" an antitrust suit with the NFL but was awarded the modest sum of $1, effectively ending the USFL and causing a scramble for its best players. Those players—like Kelly—who were originally drafted by NFL franchises, became the property of those franchises. Real estate tycoon and professional celebrity Donald Trump, then owner of the USFL's New Jersey Generals, was the impetus behind the suit and also behind the move to compete head-to-head with the NFL in the fall, which couldn't be viewed as anything but corporate suicide. The feeling was that if the NFL crushed the USFL, it would absorb the most successful franchises into the fold, thereby giving Trump his entrée into the fraternity of NFL owners and the validation that comes with it.

✿ ✿ ✿

Bock distinguished himself in the USFL primarily by playing both ways and collecting a sack in a 1984 matchup with the Memphis Showboats. Though he was playing almost exclusively as a long snapper and a back-up center by then, Bock was a two-year letterman at Virginia as a defensive tackle and looked more than comfortable rushing the passer.

I find a tape of the Houston Gamblers at Michigan Panthers matchup from 1984, when the USFL was at its apex and the Panthers were drawing (and arguably, playing) better than their NFL counterparts, the Detroit Lions. The tape is a prime piece of USFL history, as the Gamblers ran a then-experimental run-and-shoot offense designed by a coach named Mouse Davis that featured Jim Kelly sprinting out and hitting a passel of tiny wide receivers who improvised their routes on the fly.[4] Oddly though, in this game, they move the ball primarily via white running back Todd Fowler, who in this particular game is being made to look like Walter Payton by a Panthers defense that expected Kelly to throw the ball forty-five to fifty times. The score stands at 28–21, Michigan, in the fourth quarter.

Part of Kelly's USFL "tryout" involved throwing passes to Gamblers owner Jerry Argovitz, during which he broke one of Argovitz's fingers. Kelly was essentially given "carte blanche" by the USFL to pick which franchise he wanted to play for, and he chose Houston, where he could play indoors in a pass-first offense, which proved to be a prescient choice being that the Houston run-and-shoot prepared him so well to run the K-gun offense in Buffalo. This (the carte blanche for elite players) was part of how the USFL managed to snatch key players away from the NFL in this era.

This tape has commercials included, which is in itself a fascinating walk down "products that no longer exist/matter" memory lane, including AT&T phone service, Oldsmobile, and the IBM personal computer, which was billed as "a tool for modern times" in an elaborate ad featuring Charlie Chaplin and roller skates. There was also a weird Lowenbrau commercial that featured a bunch of middle-aged guys in suits playing pickup basketball over a weird Lowenbrau-themed ballad backing track. What was pretty awesome though, unironically, was the Hewlett-Packard marketing a touchscreen computer in 1984, though it would take nearly thirty more years before the general public was comfortable using this technology.

It also features two of the more entertaining kickers in USFL history in Novo Bojovic (Panthers) and Toni Fritsch (Gamblers). Bojovic was born in Yugoslavia and kicked in the era when having a foreign, soccer-style kicker seemed to be a pro football core value. Fritsch had a standout soccer career in Austria, and then kicked for the Cowboys, Chargers, Oilers, and Saints after being discovered by Tom Landry in 1971. By 1984, he was quite rotund and wore his face mask so low that it looked like another chin strap.

Detroit had Bobby Hebert and Anthony Carter, offensively, in addition to future Buffalo Bills standout Ray Bentley on the defensive side. Defensive end Larry Bethea and linebacker John Corker harass Kelly in the pocket for the duration of the quarter. Fowler plows across the goal line late in the fourth quarter to pull Houston to within one. Bock takes the field again for the game-tying point-after-touchdown (PAT).

The Gamblers take over again with 1:24 to go with the score tied. On yet another sprint draw, Fowler rumbles for nearly twenty more yards against a defense that seems unwilling or unable to yet acknowledge him. Kelly then hits future Redskin Ricky Sanders in the flat. Kelly has thus far thrown for a modest (for him) 210 yards with a pair of scores and a pair of picks. Later in the drive he is sacked on successive plays by Reggie Singletary and future replacement Ram Kyle Borland. The Gamblers face thirty and twenty with forty-five seconds remaining and try to fool the Panthers with a draw to Fowler. It doesn't work, bringing up a fourth a long, with Joe Bock back on the field for an important punt snap.

Overtime[5] begins with Novo Bojovic line-driving a squib kick into a Houston Gambler, which (squib) is recovered by Michigan. However, the Gamblers held, and on his next series Kelly drives the Gamblers down the field into Toni Fritsch field goal range, including a key scramble for a first down. The broadcast then cuts to a shot of the fat, balding

Austrian reclining on the Gambler bench, looking as though he is about
to fall asleep. Fritsch and Bock trot onto the field for what could be the
game-winning field goal. I've snapped in those situations and to say that
it's a miserably pressure-filled moment would be an understatement.

The snap is perfect, but the kick is blocked by the 6'6" John Corker.

Eventually, the diminutive and Yugoslavian Bojovic kicks the game-
winner for Michigan, and I'm struck by how unusual it is to see an
enthusiastic crowd and a winning team in the Pontiac Silverdome.

❖ ❖ ❖

The 1986 season for Bock was a wash from a football standpoint:
"Though I did play one game," he recalls. "I played flag football for a
team called 'Otto's Hots' in Rochester. It was in a rough eight-on-eight
league with playoffs and a national championship and everything. Otto's
Hots advanced through to the championship game, which is when they
brought me in. Before the game I could tell there was some controversy
with the other team and the officials. The other team was screaming
that we had a 'ringer' and couldn't play. I said to my teammates, 'We've
got a ringer? Who'd they bring in, Jim Kelly or something?' But they
were like, 'No, dumbass, it's *you*!'"

Friends warned Bock that he would get his "face bloodied" playing
sandlot flag football, which almost proved prophetic. "The nose tackle
tried to break my nose on the last play of the game, which was a kneel-
down," he recalls. "He took a run at me with his forearm; I said a little
prayer and dipped down, and his elbow grazed the top of my head."

Little did Bock know, more significant travails awaited him in the
NFL.

Good but not marquee USFL players like Bock were left to scramble for NFL opportunities. One coach, Hank Kuhlmann, who was with
Bock in Birmingham, called him "the best long snapper I've ever seen."
It was as a traveling meat salesman that Bock knocked on opportunity's
door in Buffalo. Or, more literally, he knocked on head coach Marv
Levy's door every Monday morning. The humbling nature of playing
professional football at a high level for three years and then having to
sell meat out of a truck to many of your peers doesn't escape me. The
fact that Bock was able to compartmentalize this in his psyche is the
object of much interest for me.

"I would drive up to Buffalo and sell steak and fish to a lot of the Bills players for personal use," Bock recalls. Rich Stadium—now called "Ralph Wilson Stadium"—is nestled in the middle of a residential area in Orchard Park, New York, which feels more like a college town. Working on a book project with Jim Kelly, I drove the same roads, parked in the same lots, and walked down the same "Players Only" ramp that Bock must have walked down, with cartons of meat in hand—well within view of the bright green turf and blue seats that must have beckoned to him, just out of reach. It's a fine line that separates glamour and humbly scraping by. That line is nowhere more evident than in the life of the fringe professional athlete.

Finally, Levy answered the door and signed Bock for the league minimum before a May minicamp, vowing to "find the best long snapper out there" if he had to go through "fifty or sixty guys" to find him. Bock, never at a loss for confidence, vowed to be that snapper. Wanting to show the Bills his work ethic, Bock would leave Rochester each morning at 4 a.m. in order to be the first player in the weight room when it opened at 6 a.m.

And then he had the preseason of his life—snapping the ball perfectly in each game and flying downfield to make tackles, which is a point of pride. "My background is in defense, Ted," he explains. "I was a linebacker and defensive end at Virginia, and I like tackling people."

After each preseason game, Levy would single Bock out for praise, saying things like "Eleven kick opportunities and eleven perfect snaps for Joe Bock." Bock surmises that Levy was trying to publicly sell, to the team, the idea of a full-time long snapper on the roster.

And then, as abruptly as it started, it was over. "Levy called me into his office right at the end of training camp and said, 'We're not keeping a snapper. Thanks for coming in.'" Bock was devastated, but he had a young family and bills to pay. Pride had to be swallowed, and he was back in the meat truck the following weekend, selling to Bills players and fans. Oh, and the Bills did keep a long snapper named Adam Lingner, who played thirteen seasons in the league and appeared in four Super Bowls. Not coincidentally, Lingner was originally drafted by the Kansas City Chiefs in the ninth round, where he played under Marv Levy.

This phenomenon—the feeling of having to watch someone lead the life that you feel you are supposed to lead—can be one of the most painful and embittering things imaginable. And Bock certainly experienced those emotions as he embarked on life's grind while another player dressed in his locker room, walked down his tunnel, and lived his dreams in front of his hometown fans.

"I had great rapport with [backup quarterback and holder] Frank Reich and Scotty Norwood, who is one of the best people in the world," he says. "Who knows if it would have made a difference in the 'wide right' field goal in Super Bowl XXV?"

Super Bowl XXV is considered to be a classic back and forth battle between teams with two disparate styles. The smashmouth Parcells-coached Giants controlled the ball and the clock via a punishing running game, while the up-tempo Bills used the K-gun offense to keep pace. The Bills had an opportunity to win the game on a last-second field goal, which they missed. It was the first in a run of Bills Super Bowl losses in the 1990s making them, oddly, a truly great team but a truly great team that is remembered primarily for what it couldn't do.

Lingner is generally held above reproach for "wide right," but one never knows. I ask Bock how he has dealt with this, over time, and he is silent for a few moments (rare for him).

"Forgiveness is such a huge key to life," he says. "Without it I would have never gotten through that. I had to get to a point of forgiveness." It should be noted that it can take a long time to arrive at that point, and that it's also a point that may need, throughout life, to be re-arrived at.

A few weeks later, Bock was contacted by the Bills again, this time to gauge his availability in the event of the looming players' strike. "They told me, 'There's gonna be a strike, and we want you to come in,'" he recalls. "I told them I'd do it, but they were only gonna pay me three hundred bucks to come in and practice all week. I said I'd do it if I can show up for Saturday's practice, snap on Sunday, and keep selling steaks during the week." Bock was making "a couple hundred bucks a day" selling steaks and couldn't afford to lose the income.

Bock says he wasn't afraid of reprisals from his Bills friends and teammates for crossing the picket line, even though union rhetoric league-wide was reportedly loud, often crazy, and very public. "It was far from nuts or crazy," he explains. "[Bills nose tackle] Freddy Smerlas was a friend of mine and loved me to death. He was saying a lot of things in the media, but I knew it would be okay because those are a great bunch of guys, which is why they were so successful."

Still, when push came to shove, Bock signed with Gene Stallings and the replacement St. Louis Cardinals, but not without conflicted feelings. "I could sure use the $5,000–$6,000 per game they were offering, because at the time I was a hundred grand in debt on my business. I'm still kicking myself for signing."

As soon as he touched down in St. Louis, Bock's wife called to relay a message from the Minnesota Vikings and his former USFL coach, Rollie Dotsch, who at the time was battling cancer. "I felt loyal to the Cardinals because they had bought my plane ticket out," Bock explains, regretful that he didn't investigate the Minnesota opportunity further. He stayed and signed in St. Louis.

Stallings, who was reared in the Bear Bryant tradition of tough, Southern, and ultraserious football coaches intended to use Bock to replace incumbent snapper Mike Morris during the strike. "My goal was to make Gene Stallings laugh or smile just once," Bock recalls. Bock played well in his first game again against Washington, snapping perfectly and flying downfield to collect a couple of tackles. So well, in fact, that Morris came "flying back in" for his job. Stallings activated Morris but kept Bock on the inactive list. Seeing his NFL dream slipping away, he felt restless and conflicted.

"I couldn't stand to go to the stadium that second week and watch somebody do what I perceived as my job," he says. "Instead of going to the game that week, I toured the Budweiser brewery in town."

A knock on his meeting-room door the following week changed Bock's fate and made him a historic oddity. Figuring he was being released, Bock collected his playbook and started to say his goodbyes to the rest of the offensive linemen. Instead, Stallings pulled him out to let him know that Marv Levy and the hometown Bills wanted him back, via trade.

"Marv Levy wants to trade for you," said the stoic Stallings. "I told Levy I'd leave it up to you. We like having you here, but I can't guarantee you a job."

"I've been up to the Arch, toured the breweries, and been to the World Series," Bock replied. "It's time to go home." For the first time, his coach cracked a smile. Bock even offered to stay in town and play on the Cardinals' "scout" defense in practice while the trade was being finalized. When I ask him the terms of the deal, for whom he was traded, Bock replies, "I was traded for a hundred bucks."

✿ ✿ ✿

After the trade, Bock arrived in Buffalo following the Bills' Wednesday practice, which is, as any ex-player knows, the first "real" practice of the week. When he arrived at the facility he was greeted by a player named Mark Walczak, who happened to be the guy Bock was replacing on the roster.

"Mark was just a kid out of college, but he introduced himself," Bock recalls. "And then he said, 'Hey, are you going back to Rochester? I could use a lift.'" As it turns out, Rochester's only two NFL long snappers shared a ride home that evening. "He was very cool about it," Bock recalls. "I hope I was nice about it, too." Walczak would land on his feet, spending time with the Indianapolis Colts and then logging five years as a San Diego Charger, where he would become star linebacker Junior Seau's roommate, confidant, and best friend.

Bock's final NFL game would come against the New York Giants and game-changing outside linebacker Lawrence Taylor, who by then had crossed the picket line. "It was a comedy of errors," says Bock. "By far the worst game in NFL history . . . it had interceptions, fumbles, and Lawrence Taylor all over the place."

Bock's roommate was starting replacement center Will Grant, who had already logged ten years in the league but knew he would have his hands full with Lawrence Taylor (LT). "Will said, 'I'm gonna get in a fight with LT on the first play and get thrown out so that you have to block him the rest of the way,'" Bock recalls, explaining that when facing the 4-3 defense the center was uncovered and often had to pick up a blitzing linebacker, which against the Giants meant chasing LT all over the field. Grant, to say the least, was struggling with the future Hall of Famer.

"Marv Levy starts yelling at Will at halftime, saying 'You've been called for holding six times!' to which Will replied, 'Is that all? I'm holding him on every play!'"

A 3–3 tie through four quarters, the game went into overtime, where the Bills had two opportunities to kick winning field goals. "We had a field goal attempt on third down," says Bock. "I fired a perfect snap to holder Dan Manucci, who dropped it, after which Lawrence Taylor flew in and smothered both the holder and the kicker. The next play, on fourth down, we lined up for another one. Again, I fired back a perfect snap and Manucci dropped that one, too. On the sidelines they were auditioning holders between plays."

With three minutes remaining in overtime, the Bills began a drive that would stall deep inside Giants territory with twenty-seven seconds remaining. Levy called for the field goal team and again sent Dan Manucci out as his holder. "We line up, and I look over my head and see '56' [Taylor] lined up over me," Bock remembers. "I said to myself, 'I gotta come up with a plan,' which as it turned out was to say a prayer, look up again, and hope I'd misread the jersey. That didn't work, so I had to come up with a Plan B. I said, 'Hey LT, what are you doing inside? You've been rushing from the outside all night.' He didn't say a word because he never said a word to anybody on the field. I decided on Plan C, which was to tell a joke right before the snap to try to get him to hesitate. So I said, 'Hey Manucci, better not drop this one, I might be right behind it!' After the snap, I popped up and LT was just standing there. I stood next to him and watched the ball sail through the uprights. I said to him, 'Bills 6, Giants 3; it's in the books.' He didn't say anything in response. He just shook my hand and walked off the field."

"I don't tell many people that story," he says. "It's one of my special favorites.

"After the game I had a bunch of reporters around me because of the Rochester thing. I still had all my gear on, and the first thing one of them said was, 'Hey, Joe, Fred Smerlas said you'll never sell a box of steak or seafood in here again if you play during the strike.'"

Bock was disappointed that the media was trying to stir up dissension within the Bills.

"I said, 'I don't believe it to be true, and I don't think it's true, but if it is, tell Freddy he'll never eat that good again!'

"A week later, I'm in the locker room and Freddy is in his underwear signing trading cards for my clients' kids."

3

FULL METAL JACKET
The Coach: Les Steckel

Former NFL head coach and longtime assistant Les Steckel is always on message. "I raise money for a living," he explains, now president of the Fellowship of Christian Athletes. Steckel, a former Marine, is also often right. In addition to serving as an infantryman in Vietnam, Steckel was a Golden Gloves boxing champion at the University of Kansas. Like many coaches, he has crisscrossed the country following the next job. He was an assistant at the University of Colorado, an assistant at Navy, and then with the San Francisco 49ers. After several years as an assistant under the legendary Bud Grant with the Minnesota Vikings, he was promoted to head coach before the 1984 season. He emphasized military-style discipline, and the professionals under his charge struggled to a 3–13 record. Minnesota fans hoisted homemade signs that read, "Less Steckel, More Bud," in an effort to lure Grant out of retirement.

I sought Steckel, however, because I was an admirer of his offensive philosophy. Steckel's greatest piece of coaching work was with the 1999 Tennessee Titans, where he coordinated an offense led by a bruising running attack featuring Eddie George running behind the NFL's best lead-blocking fullback in Lorenzo Neal. The offense lacked an elite quarterback (they had a good-not-great Steve McNair) and an elite wide receiver (their best was probably Derrick Mason) but got it done with sound run-game principles: a great offensive line which included Bruce Matthews and Brad Hopkins, and a versatile tight end in Frank

Wycheck. His team seemed to be built on the Parcells model of run game, ball control, and defense and was good enough to advance through the playoffs, knocking off the AFC team of the 1990s (Buffalo), a Peyton Manning–led Indianapolis Colts squad, and the Jacksonville Jaguars en route to a Super Bowl, which they lost to the St. Louis Rams by one inch, as wide receiver Kevin Dyson was tackled an inch short of the goal line, saving a storybook Super Bowl title for Kurt Warner and the Rams. Steckel then assumed the same role in 2000, leading a very similar (defense-and-run game, no elite quarterback) Tampa Bay offense to a playoff appearance.

One of his proudest coaching projects, however, concerned guiding the future of a former Heisman Trophy winner and an American phenomenon.

"I used to play basketball with Doug Flutie at the Natick YMCA," he recalls. "There were three courts, and the first one was always reserved for the studs—guys who had played in college and so forth. That's where Flutie always played. Nobody could guard him, and when the game was on the line, his teammates would just give him the ball and clear out of the way. He was one of the best natural athletes I've ever seen."

Flutie and Boston College (BC) dueled with Bernie Kosar's Miami Hurricanes in a nationally televised game in 1984 that, like all Miami games in that era, became something of a "good vs. evil" morality play, inasmuch as Boston College was a collection of "gritty white guys" and Miami, by that time, was known for wearing military fatigues to games, slush funds, and swaggering end-zone dances. Anyway, Flutie won the game on a long pass to Gerald Phelan, was on the cover of *Sports Illustrated,* and pretty much single-handedly gave BC a national reputation, so much so that a phrase called "The Flutie Effect" was coined that describes the phenomenon wherein a school does something noteworthy athletically and then sees a significant uptick in enrollment and alumni donations. Another reason to like Flutie: he was a finalist for the Rhodes Scholarship.

Flutie, however, was at something of a career crossroads when he and Steckel crossed paths. A Heisman Trophy winner and a national sports icon for his "Hail Mary" at Boston College, Flutie was especially deified in the Northeast but found the professional game to be a tougher adjustment. After playing for the USFL's New Jersey Generals, he landed for parts of two seasons in Chicago with Mike Ditka, where he was never accepted into a clubhouse that was loyal to its own brash leader, Jim McMahon, and popular backup, Mike Tomczak. Flutie was openly ridiculed by his teammates for both his size and his close relationship with Ditka. Flutie was 5"9", which is tiny by pro quarterback standards and makes Flutie the "outlier" of all statistical "outliers" from a size perspective.[1] Without the Hail Mary and the subsequent Heisman Trophy, Flutie probably goes down in history as just another great college quarterback who was something of a local athletic legend. Still, Flutie clearly had a pretty outstanding set of "intangibles" and it makes you wonder how many other "Fluties" have fallen through the cracks over the years.

Ditka traded Flutie to New England during the 1987 strike, where Flutie joined a crowded and already-chummy quarterback room that included former 1983 first-round pick, Tony Eason, longtime Patriot Steve Grogan, and three-year UCLA starter Tom Ramsey. Eason had started in a Super Bowl in 1986, but was undersized and drafted by a coach (Ron Meyer) who didn't really want him. He has the distinction, along with Todd Blackledge, of being one of the 1983 quarterback crop that didn't really pan out. Grogan had the luxury of being perhaps the most popular person in town—the long-suffering backup to an inconsistent starter. "Steve Grogan was maybe the toughest guy to ever play the position," says Steckel.

Once again, Flutie was the odd man out, but this time it was in his backyard where fans clamored for him. "Doug was ambitious and was a competitor who just wanted to get on the field," Steckel recalls. "Finally, I asked Dante Scarnecchia—who is a coaching legend in NFL circles and was our special teams coach—if he could try returning punts. Well, Flutie caught his first punt and his momentum carried him out of bounds and 60,000 fans gave him a standing ovation anyway. That's when I really realized how beloved he was in New England."

Still, there was no place for Flutie in Steckel's crowded quarterback room, and the coach knew he had to do something. "Doug created a little culture problem." Steckel suggested to Flutie that he should consider playing in Canada, telling him "you'll probably own that league," and "you'll play so well that you may end up owning a team in that league someday."

"He got extremely angry with me," says Steckel of Flutie's reaction. However, Flutie did eventually make his way to Canada, where in his career with the BC Lions and Calgary Stampeders he threw for over 41,000 yards and 270 touchdowns. Flutie passed for over 6,600 yards in a single season, which is a professional record regardless of league. The wide-open field and pass-centric nature of the Canadian game seemed to agree with Flutie, and also made his coach a prophet, as Flutie was actually part owner of a CFL franchise for a time and is so beloved in Canada that he was named an "honorary Canadian." Remarkably, after an eight-year run in the CFL, Flutie returned to the NFL where he played very capably for the Bills and the Chargers. All told, he logged twenty-one seasons as a professional quarterback between the NFL, CFL, and USFL.

✦ ✦ ✦

In 1987, Steckel was an "offensive assistant" on a coaching staff under Raymond Berry that eschewed job titles. Coaching, in addition to being incredibly intense and requiring insanely long hours, is also, oddly, relationally intimate. These are men you eat, shower, travel, and talk with constantly. The closeness is, in fact, one of the addictions that football feeds. The feeling of needing others and, in turn, being needed by them. The best coaching staffs—and the best teams—are those with stable, thriving, interpersonal dynamics.

"Raymond was the most humble, genuine, and honest person I've ever been around," he says. "He gave the players such respect and spoke with such calm. I used to get frustrated with him and ask him to get pumped up and kick a chair or something, but Raymond lived moment by moment in the Holy Spirit, and the players hung on his every word. He was the ideal Christian coach. The media was very harsh on him because of his faith, but he handled it better than anyone I've ever seen."

A six-time Pro Bowler and a member of the Pro Football Hall of Fame as a player, part of the Raymond Berry mythos includes the fact that he only dropped two passes in his entire career as the go-to receiver for Johnny Unitas and the championship-era Baltimore Colts. In thirteen seasons, he fumbled the football only once. His work ethic was legendary. Berry would need a surplus of faith and interpersonal skill to handle the fracturing Patriot locker room at the beginning of the 1987 strike.

"There were a lot of old former NFL players on our 1987 staff," says Steckel. The staff was populated with many no-nonsense old-school NFL names like Ed Khayat,[2] Don Shinnick, and Jimmy Carr—who between them had over thirty years of NFL playing experience. "There was a tremendous amount of disappointment in the striking players because, when they played, our coaches didn't fly first class and played for a few thousand bucks—essentially for the love of the game. It was a sea of emotion and hostility."

In reality, nationwide, the coaching profession was on the beginning edge of a cultural shift that is still taking place today. "So many coaches wanted to be Bear Bryant and Vince Lombardi," Steckel said. "I initially said that the last thing I wanted to be was a coach because I felt like all they did was berate guys and curse at them. I never wanted to be that guy."

The 1987 strike put old-school coaches at odds with new-school players, and the result, at least in New England, was unpleasant. "The regular players would throw eggs on our cars in the lot when we were driving to meetings with the replacements, but I maintained contact with our regulars. I told them that I saw the strike as a separation in a marriage, but I wasn't about to get divorced from my players. I knew it was gonna be over."

Steckel, who has somehow logged thirty years in the Marine Corps and retired as a colonel, remembered the previous strike in 1982—and was in fact allowed to go on active duty by Vikings coach Bud Grant. It was the previous experience that gave him the sense that the clock was ticking on the 1987 strike.

"It felt like college coaching all over again, in that we were recruiting players," he recalls. "We had a handful of training camp cuts—guys that had been with us before. We had guys who knew guys who wanted to play, and we even had a few tryouts, but we had to move quickly."

Steckel found himself coaching—and mentoring—young, inexperienced players who had to adjust to pro football life on and off the field.

"We had a replacement quarterback, a Christian guy, who called from the hotel the night before a game and said, 'Coach, there are all kinds of girls here who are running around with their clothes off.' There was an onslaught of girls who just wanted to go to bed with an NFL player—they didn't care if he was a replacement or a regular."

The strike did provide an opportunity for at least one Patriot quarterback to cross the line and make a difference. "Flutie showed up halfway through the strike and was a tremendous asset," Steckel remembers.

Perhaps Flutie's finest hour as a Patriot came in the team's final replacement game—a 21-7 victory over the Houston Oilers in the Astrodome. "We had to minimize the offense for running purposes," says Steckel. "I remember taking the bus through Houston to the Astrodome. This was right after the oil crash of 1987, and there was nobody in the streets and certainly nobody at the game."

"The replacements knew the strike wasn't gonna last long, and the majority just said 'thank you so much for this once-in-a-lifetime opportunity,'" he says. "There was no animosity or anger when they left." Though, of the strike, Steckel says, "I don't know what it accomplished."

With an 8-7 record, the Patriots narrowly missed the playoffs in 1987. After two more mediocre seasons, Berry was eventually fired by new owner Victor Kiam after he wouldn't relinquish player personnel duties.

"Raymond Berry was the finest Christian man I ever met, and I didn't even see it," Steckel recalls, on a career that saw him fired a dozen times and took his family on a journey through twelve moves to thirteen different states. "Berry had to fire me," he says, on the end of his tenure in New England, "but I would have fired myself. I was a highly ambitious, driven man. I was so aggressive. I wanted to run the show."

4

WHO WILL YOU RUN TO?

The New Irving Fryar: Larry Linne

When Larry Linne made his NFL debut in 1987, I was eleven years old. My days involved riding my bike to Hook's Drugstore with Mitch Warner, where we would purchase football cards and cans of white paint, which we would then use to line a football field onto a vacant lot behind his home. All of this, especially the phrase "vacant lot," sounds unspeakably quaint in the way that the stories my father used to tell about his childhood also sounded unspeakably quaint. We live in a world now where kids text one another rather than picking up a rotary dial phone[1] in the kitchen. We live in a world where we don't quite feel comfortable letting our children ride all over town on their bikes and where pro athletes feel that much less accessible, in spite of the fact that their mostly ordinary thoughts are all over Twitter.

The year 1987 was mullets,[2] gold chains, boom boxes (which we called "ghetto-blasters"), Def Leppard cassette tapes, trips to the public pool, and Air Jordans. Instead of checking our phones for the weather report before going out to play, we called "time and temperature," which was a phone number that would give you the time of day and the outside temperature and at the time felt like a simply stunning techno- logical advancement.

In 1987, my father and I would routinely drive the half hour to Anderson, Indiana, to watch the Colts practice in training camp at An- derson University. The crowds were small and the setting was intimate.

It wasn't unusual to find defensive coordinator Rick Venturi enjoying a prepractice cigarette next to the gate that led to the practice field. It wasn't unusual to nod hello to Venturi and get a genuine "hey fellas" in return. It also wasn't unusual for an eleven-year-old boy to get to carry the pads of NFL stars[3] back up to the gymnasium that served as the Colts' summer locker room.

Today, NFL training camps are a homogenized, league-run "experience" that loosely translated just means that there are way more people, officially licensed trinkets are everywhere and way more expensive, hip-hop music is omnipresent, and there are inflatable bounce-things for children to badger their parents about rather than actually watching the action on the field. Modern training camps are evidence of the fact that, as a culture, we are apparently phobically uncomfortable with silence and the lack of constant stimuli. Modern training camps usually take place at a team's local practice facility, as the days of packing up the operation and journeying to a local small college are mostly a thing of the past. As such, players enter and exit the field directly, making the long, languid walk with fans a thing of the past as well.

"You probably wonder how I found you and why I reached out to you for this," I say to former Patriots wide receiver Larry Linne when we finally connect.

"That was actually going to be my first question," he replies, laughing.

I go on to tell him the story about the Foxboro turf and the obscure indoor league, which led me to the DVD of his first game against the Browns, which led us to this interview. He gives a deep belly laugh.

"Life has been an interesting evolution," he explains, before telling me the story of an out-of-work young father who took an opportunity to suit up during the strike, who is now the owner of the largest insurance consulting firm in the United States and a twice-published author of books on brand marketing. To say that Linne has done well for himself would be an understatement; however, it's the "how" that is of the most interest. There's a refreshing humility about Linne, which is in contrast to the approach of some "self-made men" who seem to want to let you know exactly how fabulous they are and how they got to be that fabulous. Football is nothing if not humbling for most of us who are done well before we want to be.

"When I got out of college, I got a free agent shot with the Patriots," he explains. "I hung on until right before the first game of the 1987 season. When Raymond Berry cut me he said, 'Larry, we'd love to have you, but we just don't have the room.' My dad[4] played with Ray Berry, so I think he had an eye toward helping me out."

Before Linne's final preseason game as a Patriot against Dallas, Berry cryptically told him to play well because Dallas "had some interest." However, after Linne was released, the phone didn't ring.

"Suddenly, I was back home in Texas with a baby daughter and no job," he says. "The Cowboys were right there in town, so I decided to give them a call."

The call proved valuable, as Dallas brought Linne in as a practice player, and for a week and a half before the strike, he was a Dallas Cowboy. Then the strike happened and, inexplicably, Linne refused to become a replacement Cowboy. "I just didn't want to do it," he says. After his release from the Cowboys, he got an even more mysterious call from New England.

"We want you to come in and play for our replacement team," they said. "We already know the outcome of the strike, and we already know it will only last three weeks. But if you come in, we'll keep you for the rest of the season."

What the Patriots were cryptically describing was what would come to be known as the "practice squad" on which teams routinely carry a handful of players they don't have room for on the regular roster but would like to keep around. This was another prescient move by the NFL, for it provided a way to make the replacement games "matter" as fans could speculate as to which strike players might stick around.

Linne signed with New England, knowing that he had a full-time commitment and that the players he was replacing would, in a matter of weeks, become his teammates. But the experience was not without drama.

"They did a couple of things I thought were downright crappy," he explains. "They put me in Irving Fryar's jersey[5] [number 80] just to piss him off and try to lure him back in." Fryar was one of the few offensive stars New England boasted in the mid-1980s, along with running backs Craig James and Tony Collins. Their best player, in fact, was offensive guard John Hannah.

If Patriots head coach Raymond Berry was the archetypal 1950s wide receiver—humble, quiet, hardworking, and efficient—his player, Irving Fryar, represented a newer, flashier, and more outspoken NFL receiver. Berry's Hall of Fame career was built on a legendary work ethic, which helped him overcome marginal speed and one leg that was markedly shorter than the other. He would routinely spend hours after practice catching football after football to improve his hands and timing. A Nebraska standout gifted with game-changing speed, Irving Fryar could take the top off an NFL secondary but was also equally capable of confounding his coaches with inconsistency and off-the-field issues. In fact, he famously made a public appearance during the players' strike in a Rolls Royce, intending to send the message that he would be okay, financially, in spite of the strike. Fryar often overpromised and underdelivered in New England, and would enjoy the majority of his pro success later in his career with the Dolphins and the Eagles.[6]

Larry Linne was more "Raymond Berry" than "Irving Fryar" in terms of his approach to the game, which may explain (in part) Berry's determination to help the young receiver get established. As did the fact that, for better or worse, the replacement games counted in the NFL standings, and while he possessed a 27–15 record in four years as New England's coach, he was still best known as the coach of the team that was throttled by Chicago 46–10 in Super Bowl XX.

Linne's regular season debut took place on October 4, 1987, in a largely empty Sullivan Stadium, while regular Patriots picketed outside. Resplendent in a hooded sweatshirt, jean jacket, and several days of stubble, regular quarterback Tony Eason looked semihomeless as he clutched a cup of coffee. One of Boston's biggest professional sports stars, Roger Clemens, was pitching across town in Fenway Park, looking for his twentieth win of the season.

New England lineman Steve Moore wore a sandwich board that read "Justice on the Job" and "Freedom of Choice Denied NFL Players." Though it was ironic given his salary compared to that of the average fan, Moore's board spoke to the level of free agency and player movement that players enjoy today, wherein they are free to move about and seek the best deal once their initial contract expires. The result is often a bidding war for the services of athletes, which keeps the NFL in the news in the off-season and makes athletes richer, but makes it rare for a player to start and finish his career with one team. Regardless, on the field on October 4, 1987, most of the players were making their pro debuts.

"It's like a lab experiment," says analyst Bob Trumpy, of replacement football. "Just put two or three ingredients together and hope there's not an explosion."

On the sideline wearing a bright red Patriots parka over a ball cap, Raymond Berry looks oddly infantile, as it's the kind of hooded parka which has drawstrings that tie in a bow just under the wearer's chin. His face bears an expression of pain and unease.

His counterpart across the field, Marty Schottenheimer, was also an NFL player and was, in some ways, linebacking's version of Berry—gritty, hardworking, and overachieving. He says, of the strike, "We don't have time to feel sorry for ourselves. I can't worry about who's here. I'm a football coach and that's what I'm doing." Schottenheimer's staff includes a young secondary coach named Bill Cowher, fresh off his own career as a journeyman NFL linebacker, and just embarking on a coaching career that will see him coach in multiple Super Bowls as the head coach of the Pittsburgh Steelers.

While the Patriots have a handful of regular players on hand, Cleveland didn't have anyone cross the picket line and fields a squad made entirely of replacements who are each making a uniform $5,000 per game to suit up. Among the Cleveland replacements are Derek Tennell (tight end) and Perry Kemp (wide receiver), who will go on to enjoy poststrike NFL careers. Players from both teams come into the first replacement game having had a minimum of contact in practice, as teams were concerned with the prospect of losing yet more players to injury. By and large both rosters are populated with good, experienced players who have logged years in the USFL, CFL, and NFL camps, but they're still players who haven't hit anyone in a long, long time.

A running back named Chuck McSwain, wearing Craig James' number 32 jersey, returns the opening kickoff. There are three regular players—Tony Collins, Guy Morriss, and Sean Farrell—who have crossed the line. Collins, who hasn't practiced in ten days, fumbles on the game's first play from scrimmage. The fumble is an ominous harbinger of things to come as the elusive Collins[7] will put the ball on the carpet again several plays later. Fortunately for New England, the turnover is negated by a Cleveland penalty.

Collins was a Pro Bowler in 1983, but his career was marred and cut short by drug abuse, and by 1987 he was a complementary player to James. He last played in 1993 as a member of the Miami Hooters[8]

Quarterback Bob Bleier, cousin of Steeler legend Rocky Bleier, was employed in a family member's restaurant supply business prior to the strike. Collins ends the series with three fumbles on four carries.

Unlike places like Philadelphia and Detroit, the picket line has dispersed by midway through the first quarter—their spirits no doubt dampened by the cold rain. Still, 30,000 tickets were returned to the Patriot offices, and the empty stands indicate that not many of the 30,000 that remained were actually used. Meanwhile, Linne awaits his first NFL punt return, which is postponed due to a bad snap by former USFL lineman Mike Katolin, which skips off the carpet.

New England's early strategy seems to be "give the ball to Tony Collins on every play and hope he doesn't wear out or fumble." Fittingly, New England's second series ends when kicker Eric Schubert doinks one off the left upright. Cleveland's next possession ends in a Jeff Christensen sack and another skipped snap by Mike Katolin whose "dream come true" opportunity to suit up in the NFL is turning into a long snapper's worst nightmare.

Linne gets a step on Dejuan Robinson on a fade late in the first quarter but has the ball stripped from his possession just before hauling it in. On Cleveland's next series, Christensen scrambles for a first down to keep a drive alive, diving headfirst onto the spongy, wet turf rather than the customary quarterback's hook-slide. He'll finish the quarter with a modest two yards, passing.

New England's kicker, Eric Schubert, who was teaching seventh grade when he got the call from the Patriots, draws first blood with a field goal to open the second quarter.

Linne's first pro catch comes on a slant route near the end of the second quarter, as quarterback Bob Bleier finds a rhythm and Ray Berry seems to have found players that aren't named Tony Collins.

The white towel hanging from Linne's belt[9] is already dappled with blood, courtesy of a turf burn wrought from the Sullivan Stadium carpet. On the very next play, Bleier finds Linne sliding in the corner of the end zone for a score. Linne jumps up and spikes the ball, exuberantly, which prompts analyst Bob Trumpy to say, "Don't spike the ball; keep it!"

He adds, "You can't describe how that young man feels."

* * *

As coaches and players navigated the on-field implications of the strike, owners sought to unpack the myriad television-related issues that came from their decision to field replacement teams and air replacement games—namely, the steep drop in ratings and therefore ad revenue from companies who no longer wanted to peddle their products on what they deemed to be subpar telecasts.

A *New York Times* report published the week after the first batch of strike games would bear this out. According to the piece, "The final television ratings for the National Football League games last Sunday—the first games using replacement players—showed declines of about 20 percent from the pre-strike games."

CBS, which broadcast two games in most markets, reported an average rating of 12.2 for the first game and 9.9 for the second. The first game rating was down 17 percent; the second was down 27 percent. Each rating point equals 886,000 households. NBC drew a rating of 9.0, down 17 percent from the 10.8 it drew for the last game before the strike.

"ABC had earlier reported an even larger decline in its ratings for *Monday Night Football*. The 13.8 rating it drew last Monday was the second lowest since the show began in 1970."

"Network executives have said they were not disappointed by the ratings, largely because they expected worse."[10]

"We've built up a good relationship with the networks over twenty-five years," said Browns owner Art Modell. "We won't leave them high and dry, contract or no contract."

His interviewer, Bob Costas, explained that network commentators were taking varied approaches to the replacement games. Some were "tongue and cheek" and some "critical." Costas wondered how the owners would respond to honest critiques of the product on the field.

"We think these games could very well be competitive," said Modell, as noncommittally as possible. "We want to end this thing [strike] and the best way to end this thing is to continue to play . . . all sides lost a total of $250 million in 1982 . . . I feel a deep sense of loss in that this is my fourth strike. I thought the strike in 1982 was the strike to end all strikes. I don't understand the issues, I don't understand why they're striking, and the quicker they all come back, the better we're all gonna be."

Modell was quoted in a preseason *Athlon's Pro Football* interview saying, "We can't afford another strike. We're still recovering from the last one [1982]. I think a lot of us have to realize that there has to be some compromise in the negotiations. Neither side can get everything it wants."[11]

Modell wasn't in any way coy or evasive on his strategy: to use replacement players to manipulate the actual players into coming back as quickly as possible. On this, he explained to Costas, there was unity amongst owners. "I have never seen an ownership group as unified as we are on this issue," he explained.

He ended by saying, "This adversarial relationship with players is not something that I had in the past." He was essentially communicating a displeasure with the shifting power dynamic in professional sports— one in which the player was clamoring for a bigger say, and a bigger piece of the revenue pie. The 1950s and 1960s—the beginning of the television era—were a golden age for owners, in which revenues climbed while unagented players continued to play for less than they were worth.

❊ ❊ ❊

Back in the booth, in what had to be a first and a last in NFL history, Don Criqui opens his halftime segment with an anecdote about the tennis career of 1960s radical Abbie Hoffman, to whom he had a tangential connection. "Instead of lobs he threw bombs," says Criqui, clearly at a loss for things to talk about.

The second half opens with a modest Cleveland drive, and analyst Bob Trumpy makes light of replacement tackle Keith Bosley's knee injury, saying, "How is Cleveland going to *function* without Bosley at right tackle?" Adding, "I tell you, those two trainers are working," as Bosley is carried off the field. He is delighted with his own comedic observations and later likens Bosley's knee to "a glazed ham," prompting Criqui to reply, "You're all heart."

Linne opens his second half with a first-down reception on a curl route as Bleier's confidence in him appears to be growing. He just misses Linne on a deep fade against press coverage several plays later, Linne's bare arms scraping across the cold, wet turf as he lays out for the throw.

There are images of fans wrapped in all manner of plastic parkas and even trash bags, defending against the cold wind and rain as the second half takes on an interminable quality. There is something almost masochistic about watching and studying these games in their entirety.

A man wears a paper grocery bag over his head on which he's written "Scab Fan." It occurs to me that the bag over the head of the fan was a distinctly 1980s phenomenon. Trumpy's sarcasm reaches epic proportions as mammoth tackle Keith Bosley is removed from the field via a golf cart, saying, "My heart is broken," and "he was great while he was there." Surreal. Later, "sideline reporter" Bud Collins—who looks like a British lit professor in a beard and golf cap—interviews a passel of enthusiastic fans. "I can sympathize with them [regular players]," says the fan, "but I don't get paid $30,000 a day to play a sport. I get paid $30,000 a *year*."

The wind gusts over thirty miles per hour, making already limited passing games even more prohibitive. However, Jeff Christensen finds Perry Kemp on a corner route in the third quarter, gaining thirty yards and representing the biggest offensive play of the game for Cleveland. The Browns' offense also seems to be finding a groove behind the running of Larry Mason.

Linne's last reception of the game comes on a twelve-yard out-cut near the end of the third quarter. Replacement running back Chuck McSwain fumbles on the very next play, giving Cleveland another opportunity. Christensen finds a way to throw the ball in the wind, primarily to tight end Derek Tennell, and Cleveland eventually rides Larry Mason to a 20–10 victory. Cleveland's offensive game is, in a weird way, a perfect example of "Martyball," which is predicated on a strong running game and time of possession.

"I'm not sure fans would stand for this for three or four weeks," says Trumpy. "It would be very difficult to sell this week after week. As a novelty, it was certainly adequate."

The telecast ends with an eerie wide shot of Sullivan Stadium, over which a PA announcer intones, "We'll hope to see you next Sunday when the New England Patriots host the Buffalo Bills." Except that no one remains in the stands to hear the announcement.

Following the replacement games and true to Berry's promise, Linne would stick with the Patriots for the remainder of the 1987 season. "The Patriot players I had relationships with were very cool about the whole thing," Linne recalls. "They understood what it was like to be a jobless guy with a new kid. Even Irving Fryar was nice about it.

"There was only one guy who couldn't give it up, and that was Craig James," he says. James is noteworthy for a few reasons. One, he was part of the famous (and ethically infamous) "Pony Express" backfield at Southern Methodist University (SMU) with Eric Dickerson, pre–death penalty, at a time when cash was allegedly flowing through the doors of the SMU football building like water. He was also a white running back in the NFL in what was/is essentially the post–white-running-back era. Finally, and most recently, he was involved in a strange controversy involving his son's college football coach, Mike Leach, which may have resulted in Leach's ouster from Texas Tech and may have contributed to James's own ouster from ESPN where he was working as a college football analyst.[12]

"He made an issue out of it all season . . . he wouldn't look at me or talk to me. He had the worst attitude of anyone I've ever seen."

5

YO, BUM RUSH THE SHOW

Replacement Rams: From Suge Knight to Steve Dils

Public Enemy's debut album, *Yo, Bum Rush the Show,* debuted in April 1987 to mixed and curious reviews. Public Enemy was described as "a more serious brand of inner-city aggression" by Joe Brown of the *Washington Post.* Jon Pareles of the *New York Times* wrote that Public Enemy "marketed itself as the distillation of black anger and resistance." Their iconic logo featured the silhouette of a black man in crosshairs. Their music wasn't so much melodic as it was relentless. It provided the perfect soundtrack for a violent pursuit like professional football. In the 1980s and early 1990s, Public Enemy's songs became the de facto soundtrack for high school, college, and professional teams across the nation.

In October 1987, on the West Coast, future Death Row Records rap tycoon Marion "Suge" Knight was suiting up for the replacement Los Angeles Rams. He was a defensive tackle and a not terribly memorable one at that.

"He went by 'Marion' Knight?" asks Rams quarterback Steve Dils. "I'm not sure I remember his name . . . but then again I spent most of my time with the offensive guys."

There seemed to be two schools of thought regarding replacement quarterbacks during the strike. One, to secure an aging veteran with several years of NFL roster experience behind him (like John Reaves, Guido Merkens, or Bruce Mathison), or go with young upstarts with potential who may have been camp cuts (like Mike Hold, Shawn Hallo-ran, Mike Hohensee, and Sean Payton) and who all lack at least one quality that would make them truly enticing or valuable to an NFL club (like size or arm strength). A third category includes players like Gary Hogeboom and Jeff Kemp—veteran roster backups who were enticed to cross the line.

Steve Dils belongs in the third category. A former fourth-round pick of the Minnesota Vikings, the Stanford standout had settled in behind Jim Everett as the Rams' backup quarterback. Dils played for Bill Walsh at Stanford, where he led the Cardinal to a Bluebonnet Bowl victory in 1978 and was the recipient of the Sammy Baugh Trophy, given to the nation's top passer. He started most of the 1983 season in Minnesota before being traded to Los Angeles in 1984.

"There was so much detail to being a quarterback," Dils says. "Bill [Walsh] was so good at asking you to do the things you were good at and not asking you to do the things you weren't good at. I regularly lean on things I learned from Bill, from a leadership and management stand-point. He taught me how to make people feel included and valued. He was just a fascinating man . . . truly one in a million."

The decision on the part of the NFL Players Association to strike following Week 3 would challenge all of Dils's leadership skills, and then some.

"The thing I had to wrestle with was calling a strike after Week 3," he says. "In the NFL, guys get eight paychecks . . . paychecks that we have to make stretch over the course of the year. And if you don't play, you don't get paid. So as a result, you had a bunch of guys striking after just one paycheck. It made no sense at all from a strategy standpoint."

Unlike some other union strongholds around the league, the feeling inside the Rams was a mixture of ambivalence and pragmatism.

"There was a team vote prior to the strike," he recalls. "We were asked how many of us would be willing to strike over the issue of free agency. One player raised his hand . . . and it was Eric Dickerson, which makes sense if you're Eric Dickerson." Dickerson was one of the league's biggest stars in 1987, having broken the mythic 2,000-yard barrier and O. J. Simpson's single-season yardage record. However, he was also garnering a reputation as a bit of a malcontent and would be dealt to Indianapolis before the end of the season. Dickerson would rack up lots of yardage and individual accolades but would never enjoy playoff success or a Super Bowl victory. He was also a notorious post-season fumbler (see the 1985 Conference Championships at Chicago and 1986 Wild Card loss at Washington).

After a few days spent calling other veterans around the league, Dils made the difficult decision to cross the picket line along with veteran running back Mike Guman and star defensive back Nolan Cromwell.

"I was in my ninth year and wasn't in a position to walk away from that much money," he recalls. "I had to do what was right for my family, and at that time, playing was what was right. Shortly after I crossed, I had a lot of guys tell me that they wished they'd done the same thing. Guys who were investigating were realizing that we weren't going to win."

As a veteran and a quarterback, Dils was charged with helping to galvanize the replacement Rams, some of whom were familiar faces from camp and some of whom he had "never seen or heard of before." One replacement Ram was a professional Polynesian dancer, another was an inventor. In spite of the challenges, though, games were competitive.

"We had a few semi-talented guys, but for the most part, all of the teams were evenly matched," he says. "We all had simplified game plans, and I remember it being a lot of fun. We had a good bit of camaraderie for just being together for three weeks . . . and some of these guys were just having the time of their lives out there."

* * *

With one week of strike games in the books, media and public returns came rolling in, and often, the result wasn't pretty. *Sports Illustrated*'s elder statesman on pro football, Paul Zimmerman (aka Dr. Z) declared that scab football was "shock therapy, a chilling message from the owners to the striking players: We will give you something so utterly distasteful—games played without you—that your strike will crumble."[1]

He would, of course, prove prophetic. But after a week there was still optimism among the Players Association that replacement ball would fail and that the owners would acquiesce. "From what I hear, our scabs are getting beat 38–0," said striking Bills quarterback Jim Kelly during the Bills' first strike game. "I love it."[2]

"A joke, a parody, yes, yes, though the games did go on and the TV overnights weren't all that bad," wrote the acerbic Zimmerman. "Chalk one up for the curiosity factor. But ticket holders weren't seduced by the laugh-a-minute brand of football, and they stayed away from the stadiums. Chalk one up for good taste."[3]

On a sunny afternoon in Anaheim, the replacement Rams face the replacement Steelers in the second week of the strike. The Steelers are led by center Mike Webster, in his fourteenth year of NFL action. Webster, of course, died tragically in 2002 as one of the NFL's first acknowledged and publicized casualties of chronic traumatic encephalopathy (CTE). As a player, Webster was the NFL's ultimate soldier. Impeccably prepared, technically sound, and aggressive, if not undersized. Webster, at around 250 pounds, spanned multiple NFL eras. When he came into the league in 1974, a guy was considered "big" at 250 pounds. By 1987, the league was well into its steroid era and was routinely rolling out defensive linemen who were 280-plus pounds and athletic. The number of hard one-on-one helmet-related collisions that Webster must have had over the years—in practices and games—is almost unfathomable.

The strike-era Rams' regular defense was led by outside linebacker Kevin Greene, who would become one of the NFL's legendary pass rushers and who would also become an NFL Films legend. Greene was known for his bone-crushing hits (celebrated by the league's film department) and for quotes like, "Ain't nothing like feeling a quarterback's body crumble, man."[4] Such is the NFL's tenuous relationship with violence. What was once a sales tool has today become a public relations nightmare. How will the league continue to package and sell a violent and dangerous game that has never been more popular?

Because of cases like Webster's, and many others, the NFL has severely limited the number of contact practices that NFL teams are allowed in the off-season and during the regular season. According to Dr. Robert Cantu, cofounder of the Sports Legacy Institute, teams are only allowed to hit fourteen times in eighteen weeks. Such parameters may have saved Webster's life.

"If you're suspected or diagnosed with a concussion in the NFL, you're not allowed back until a physician and an independent neurologist not associated with the team clears you for competition," Cantu explains. In addition to changes at the pro level, there are widespread cultural changes in the game at all levels. "The total number of hits is down, and concussions are far better managed," he says.

It's cool and classic and a pleasant surprise to see Webster in this film. He was one of the first NFL linemen to roll up his sleeves in "gun show" fashion, and he looks positively small and athletic compared to the sumo wrestlers on NFL lines today. Remarkably, Webster played until 1990. The Kansas City Chiefs had originally brought him in as an assistant coach and he wound up on the field, in uniform. He would be dead just a dozen years later, his postfootball life lived in a haze of painkillers and dementia.

"Webster was often laced with a varying, numbing cocktail of medications: Ritalin or Dexedrine to keep him calm. Paxil to ease anxiety. Prozac to ward off depression. Klonopin to prevent seizures. Vicodin or Ultram or Darvocet or Lorcet, in various combinations, to subdue the general ache. And Eldepryl, commonly prescribed to patients who suffer from Parkinson's disease," wrote ESPN's Greg Garber in a chilling series published after Webster's death.[5]

"After 17 seasons in the National Football League, Webster had lost any semblance of control over his once-invincible body. His brain showed signs of dementia."[6]

In the same report, a doctor likened Webster's long football career to the equivalent of "25,000 car accidents" in terms of impact on his brain. The article explained that Webster would sometimes stun himself several times with a Taser, just to get to sleep.[7] Heartbreaking doesn't begin to describe it.

His life and death illustrate the addictive nature of football. The fact that—against all logic, and even in defiance of bodies that are crying out for us to stop—we keep doing it. Though I've spent my whole life playing and coaching it and much of my professional life celebrating it in print, I'm growing more and more convinced that football may be a fruit of the devil. It rarely ends well.

In our era there is at least lip service to a change in the culture of football, as coaches at every level are required to at least know more about the causes and diagnoses of head injuries in their players. Still, it takes a lot to change a culture.

"I think that while there has been some change in the culture outside the sport of football concerning physicians, parents, family members, et cetera, I am not sure that much has changed as to the culture within the sport itself," explains Dr. Robert Fabiano, of PAR Rehabilitation in Lansing, Michigan. "Football, by its nature, is a very aggressive if not violent sport. The contact between players, which occurs on every single play, involves high-speed velocity with tremendous muscle mass resulting in a physical force which can be very damaging. As to the 'bringing a player back,' certainly teams are now directed by sports trainers and physicians who set the standard as to when a player can return to the game. The problem is that concussions are invisible, rarely demonstrating any physically measurable change on X-ray, CT, or MRI. Consequently, we are still dependent upon the 'honor system' in terms of a player honestly reporting symptoms such as headache, fatigue, et cetera."

Webster also had the misfortune of playing in what I believe to be the worst era for helmets in the history of football. By the late 1970s, helmets like the Riddell Pac-3 had gotten very heavy but weren't yet any good. Guys between the ages of thirty-five and fifty will remember the Riddell Pac–series helmets as the ones with the little yellow (and later, white) rectangular pads that would fossilize and get rock hard anytime the temperature dipped below forty or once the helmets were a few years old. I remember sitting at my locker, feeling the little rectangular rock that would soon be digging into my forehead and thinking something along the lines of "I'm no scientist, but this can't be providing a whole lot of protection." But I then shrugged my shoulders and pulled on the helmet trusting that people—helmet manufacturers, coaches, other involved adults—knew what they were doing, when, in fact, they probably didn't.

This combination—heavy but subpar—made those helmets, and that era, very dangerous, especially when coupled with the introduction of steroids, which of course made players bigger, faster, and stronger. I'm not sure there's hope on the concussion horizon, and I worry about my son, even with the advances in helmet technology.

"Helmets today are a bit better, a bit bigger, and have a bit more padding," explains Cantu, who, for the record, doesn't necessarily agree with my "bad-helmet era" theory. "But the technology is essentially the same as it was in the 1980s. Add to that the fact that they were playing on carpeted concrete, which was a horrible surface for all parts of the body, including the head. Helmets today are incredibly good at preventing subdurals [subdural hematomas, or brain bruises] and skull fractures, but with the size and speed of players, the head is going to be whiplashed."

Preventing the whiplash is the technological challenge that seems to have doctors and engineers stumped because rendering the head immobile means taking away vision and flexibility, which means rendering football an entirely different game. While technology has improved, it will be a change in diagnosis and treatment of concussions, and a change in the culture of the game that will make the biggest difference.

"Concussions are diagnosed more frequently today and we also know much more about the potential long term effects which can result in permanent damage to the brain," says Fabiano. "Diagnostic measures rely on brief screening procedures that quickly assess mental capacity such as orientation, memory, concentration, and mental processing speed, physical capacity including balance, complaints of headache, dizziness [vestibular dysfunction], nausea, actual vomiting, sensitivity to light [photophobia], intolerance to noise or commotion [increased distractibility], blurred vision, et cetera."

* * *

Back in Anaheim, before Dils even sets foot on the field, the Rams go up 7–0 thanks to a blocked punt by veteran roster player Nolan Cromwell, which (the block) reverberates around in the cavernous and mostly empty Anaheim Coliseum. There's something sublime and sad about this walk down southern California football memory lane. The Rams' uniforms were always bright and vibrant in this era, and their modern, current uniform, with a darker blue and standard dark gold, just look like everyone else's blue and gold. The white-haired John Robinson and his staff all wear gleaming white polos with delightfully tacky Day-Glo blue Sansabelt slacks. The field is bright green and still set up for baseball, as it was shared with the California Angels. Rams crowds in this era were always a little detached and indifferent, but even more so two weeks into a strike that had made pro football surreal.

Pittsburgh's running backs—Frank Pollard and Earnest Jackson (225 and 230,[8] respectively)—are huge, and the Steelers run simple trap plays, lead plays, and outside tosses to them on their second series, moving the ball at will. Jackson is an interesting story. He gained 1,179 yards with the Chargers in 1984 and made the Pro Bowl. He was then traded to Philadelphia where he had a 1,028-yard season but managed to wind up on the wrong side of head coach Buddy Ryan's sarcasm. "I think he's a limited ballplayer," said Ryan of Jackson. He later said during a practice, "Get him out of here. Trade him for a six pack. It doesn't even have to be cold."[9]

Steelers coach Chuck Noll, however, was glad to assimilate Jackson, who helped a team that was only averaging 65.3 yards per game on the ground before his arrival, improve that number to 154.8. "Earnest Jackson did it all," said Noll. "He ran, he blocked, he did everything we asked of him. He became a tremendous asset to our football team."[10]

By contrast, Steve Bono's early quarterbacking is a comedy of errors. On one play, he has the ball swatted back in his face; he gathers it and runs around the right end, only to get highlight-film drilled by a Rams linebacker. It's the kind of clip that undoubtedly finds its way onto a blooper reel. Bono, however, goes on to a long and productive career as a high-end backup with San Francisco and Kansas City after the strike.

In fact, it doesn't take Bono long to redeem himself, throwing a perfect fade to Lyneal Alston to tie the score. It is Alston's first catch and first score.

Already, in the second week of the strike, there is evidence of an improving level of talent. Dils is joined offensively by fellow regulars Charles White and Mike Guman in the backfield. White, a former University of Southern California (USC) star beset by drug problems as a pro, wears his trademark huge shoulder pads and is more physical than I remember him. Unfortunately, he whiffs on a pass block in the Rams' first series and nearly gets Dils killed.

The Rams, more often than not, come out with Charles White deep in the backfield behind two fullbacks, just running simple toss plays that are easy for Tony Dungy's Steeler defense to diagnose and stop. This gives Bono good field position and more opportunities, and he throws a perfect strike to his tight end Danzell Lee on an out route to put Pittsburgh up 14–7.

Robinson opens the playbook a bit on the next drive as Dils runs a flea-flicker, giving to White, who laterals back to Dils, who goes deep downfield. In the red zone, however, is one of the oddities that make these games a joy to watch. When the Rams line up three-deep in the backfield (again), one of their fullbacks is thirty-six-year-old Cullen

Bryant, who Dils remembers not as a player but as a member of the Rams coaching staff as an assistant strength coach.

Bryant's presence in this game is another strange confluence of eras. Bryant's heyday was the late-1970s, when the Rams played Pittsburgh in a Super Bowl and when they had gray face masks and a roster that featured the likes of Vince Ferragamo and Jack Youngblood. He was already, arguably, nearly over the hill in 1978 when he led the Rams in rushing under coach Ray Malavasi. He would be usurped by Wendell Tyler the following season. Still, here he is, at thirty-six, in uniform against men ten to fifteen years his junior, proving that "living a dream" (as the cliché goes) is not only for the young. His appearance was apparently, though, a mystery even to his quarterback with whom he spent time in the huddle and in the backfield. He would log one carry for two yards as a replacement in Week 5 against Atlanta, but his lead blocks from the fullback position reverberate through the empty stadium.

Bryant died in 2009, making it impossible to know or quantify what this brief appearance meant to him. It may have been an opportunity to prove something to himself, or it may have just meant a few extra game checks. We'll never know.

There's something more violent and more contained, about this era. There are fullbacks and big linebackers colliding on nearly every play. There are few to no spread formations. Plays rarely move laterally. When people get wistful for this era, I understand why. Running back Charles White—in another iconic 1980s move—leaps over the defensive line for a two-yard touchdown run. The game is knotted at fourteen, and what is true (but wouldn't be said) is that this is shaping up to be a great game. If it weren't a replacement game, it would be called a "shootout."

In fact, booth analysts Fred Rogan and Dave Lapham play the telecast remarkably "straight," making me long for the buffoonery of Terry Bradshaw as well as the kind of art-house feel of the Philly/Chicago telecast where Irv Cross roamed Veterans Stadium interviewing random people. In Anaheim, the fans are quiet and seem far removed (physically) from the action, giving this game the sense that it could have just as easily taken place on a practice field or in an abandoned lot.

Midway through the second quarter, Dils is four of five for sixty-seven yards, as the Rams stay primarily on the ground with White running behind Bryant and Guman, making it reminiscent of old-school Robinson-era USC football. Dils does an effective job of working deep down the middle of the field off play action, hitting tight end James McDonald and wide receiver Stacey Mobley on successive throws. Being the 1980s, this is the era of the "workhorse" running back, and White has every Ram carry thus far—regular season carries that would have normally gone to Ram superstar Eric Dickerson. He picks up a big first down on a thirteen-yard draw play to extend the drive.

White is finally spelled by a backup running back named Jon Francis, who is the son of former Packer quarterback Joe Francis, who is most famous for being the Packer quarterback who preceded Bart Starr and the Lombardi/Packer dynasty. Francis would only spend one season with the club, in 1987, but would be kept on the active roster at the end of the strike.

Dils and the Rams enter the game at 0–3, making his decision to go for it inside the twenty late in the first half a curious one. To the surprise of absolutely nobody, White goes up and over the pile, but it is very close. The Rams have their regular placekicker, Mike Lansford,[11] but have decided not to use him. A Dils swing pass to Francis puts them inside the ten-yard line with a minute remaining. Robinson then, uncreatively, sends White blasting into the line on successive, fruitless plays. On third and goal from the one, Dils finds tight end James McDonald[12] on a drag for the score, sending the Rams into halftime up 21–14. The drive chews up eighty-four yards and more than nine minutes.

Dils begins the second half as accurately as he ended the first, on a sharp three-step quick out to Stacey Mobley. On the next play, Charles White flashes the ability that made him a Heisman winner at USC. He pounds into the middle of the line behind Bryant on another routine lead play but keeps his legs churning and emerges from the mass of humanity to outrace the Steeler defense for a 58-yard run, giving him 114 on the game. White would go on to lead the league in rushing in 1987, his finest season as a pro, collecting 1,137 yards and 11 touchdowns on the ground. He would be named Comeback Player of the Year.[13] White was obviously a beneficiary of the trade that sent Eric Dickerson to Indianapolis shortly after the strike. It was a three-way deal, consummated on Halloween day, and involved ten players. The Colts gave up their number-one pick and a pair of number twos in 1988.

The Bills sent Greg Bell to the Rams. In all, the Rams received six draft choices, which they turned into a handful of journeymen (Frank Stams, Aaron Cox, Daryl Henley) and a couple of busts (Gaston Green, Cleveland Gary).

On the following play, Dils strikes off of play action again, finding Malcolm Moore on an eleven-yard touchdown strike to put the Rams up 28–14.

While attendance around the league faltered, a Pittsburgh network affiliate ran a poll in which fans were asked if they liked replacement football. The station received over 2,300 responses, in which 96 percent of fans said that they liked the new-look Steelers.

The replacement Rams had two brothers—Kyle and Cary Whittingham—on their linebacking corps, playing for their father, Fred Whittingham, who was the Los Angeles linebackers coach. Kyle Whittingham, who was the most valuable player (MVP) of the 1981 Holiday Bowl as a linebacker at Brigham Young University (BYU), went on to play for the Denver Gold and the New Orleans Breakers of the USFL before embarking on a coaching career that would eventually lead him to the University of Utah, where he has been head coach since 2004. In 2008, Whittingham received the AFCA (American Football Coaches Association) Coach of the Year Award, as well as the Paul "Bear" Bryant Award. Another replacement Ram, Chris Pacheco, was selling radio ad time during the day and would make fifteen to twenty sales calls each day between practice and meetings.

Dils makes his only bad throw of the game in the third quarter, floating a ball late over the middle where it is picked off by Steeler Cornell Gowdy. Gowdy, prestrike, was employed as a contract specialist for U.S. Government General Services. And in another bit of surreality, Steeler running back Earnest Jackson, via the television analysts, reminds fans that he has a baseball memorabilia and card shop in Pittsburgh and that he has a 1952 Mickey Mantle for $4,000. Only on replacement Sunday.

Pittsburgh would add one more score, behind former USFL running quarterback Reggie Collier—something of a curiosity and something of a predecessor to runners including Randall Cunningham, Mike Vick, and Robert Griffin III. Mike Lansford uses his bare foot to, fittingly, end Ram scoring with a field goal to run the final score to 31–21. The game would represent something of a high-water mark for the 1987

Rams, just two seasons removed from the NFC Championship game in 1985. The tireless Charles White would record his best game as a pro, salting the game away for Los Angeles while setting personal marks for both carries and yards. In the ensuing weeks, Eric Dickerson would be traded to Indianapolis. Would White's performance in this game convince Robinson—to whom he already had a USC-related sentimental connection—to pull the trigger on the Dickerson deal? It's hard to say for sure.

Robinson was effusive in his praise for Dickerson in the preseason, saying, "Eric Dickerson is still a great runner. And he has so much to look forward to. I have no worries about Eric. Why should I?"[14] Adding, "Eric Dickerson has won the big game for us and he's going to win more big games. There's just no question about it."[15]

Dickerson would win a few big games; he would just do it in an Indianapolis uniform in 1987. He helped lead the Colts to an AFC East title under head coach Ron Meyer—a rare bright spot for a starless franchise that had been accustomed to losing since the departure of Bert Jones. However, that title would essentially represent the peak of Dickerson's team-related success. He would never appear in a Super Bowl.

✿ ✿ ✿

There was an interesting dynamic unfolding around the league in which elite teams, like Bill Parcells and the New York Giants, were slow to sign replacement players, as they didn't want to further upset their striking regulars. "The Giants were coming off a Super Bowl year," said Ernie Accorsi in *The GM*. "And George Young [Giants General Manager] was adamant that he'd rather lose all of the replacement games than risk alienating one of the real players. As you might expect then, the Giants did lose them all."[16]

The Giants, who were already sliding at 0–3 through three weeks of the season, also lost their first two replacement games and sat, shockingly, at 0–5. The strike was shaping the season's story line, but it was unclear even to the players as to what good would come of it.

Several of the replacement Cincinnati Bengals, including starting quarterback Dave Walter, running back Dana Wright, and defensive tackle Bill Berthusen, came from the bottom half of the New York

Giants 1987 draft. Incidentally, there was an inordinate number of good players who came out of the later rounds of the 1987 draft, including defensive end Fred Stokes (Round 12), quarterback Don Majkowski (Round 10), and running back Merril Hoge (Round 10). This was also the draft in which the Raiders locked down Bo Jackson in Round 7.

"We [players] did get some things out of the strike," says Dils, who now finds himself on the management side of the table in the commercial real estate industry. "But nobody really liked the outcome. I didn't like being forced to make a choice between staying with my team and doing what was right for my family, and I know the owners didn't particularly like having to put replacement players on the field for three weeks. But I think the strike laid the groundwork for better relations between the players and the owners moving forward. And now they [players] have it [free agency]."

Unfortunately, from a team perspective, the Rams unraveled a bit after the strike ended. Dils says that reaction by his striking teammates, within the clubhouse, was "mixed." "The majority of the guys got over it quickly," he says, "but there were a few guys who wouldn't talk to us for the rest of the year."

Unlike some of his colleagues who have struggled with postconcussion symptoms and a rocky postfootball adjustment, Dils seems remarkably self-aware and content, although he does keep up to speed on the NFL's latest public relations challenges—concussions and the dispensation of painkillers to hurting players.

"Early on it was all about getting you back on the field, and for that matter I'm not sure anyone had any clue about concussions and their long-term effects," he says. "There's a difference between what would have been diagnosed as a concussion back then and what is diagnosed today."

Dils also theorizes that certain equipment advances have actually hurt players in the long run. In 1978, when he came in with Minnesota, Dils wore a suspension helmet, which is essentially the hard plastic shell with which we're familiar, except that the inside had a series of heavy fabric strips that were suspended (hence, the name) away from the plastic, thus providing a layer of air keeping the player's head from the outer shell. "People pick up that old helmet and they can't believe I wore it," he says. Newer helmets—though infused with the latest in padding and protective advances—weigh a ton by comparison and can give players a false sense of invincibility. Also, the heavy helmet becomes a formidable weapon when it is on the shoulders of a 250-pounder who can run in the 4.5s.

"It's a violent game," he says, "but we all knew what we were getting into. We knew what the deal was. Still, it's a great game. You hate to tell someone *not* to play it."

6

WALL STREET: MONEY NEVER SLEEPS

Leigh Steinberg

Very rarely do I get nervous before conducting an interview. I was nervous before briefly interviewing Michael Jordan in his last year in the NBA when I was in my mid-twenties. I was nervous before attending a Mike Tyson *press conference.*

I'm nervous before talking with Leigh Steinberg, I think, because of the sheer volume of impact he's had on pop culture and professional sports, and the fact that the Jerry Maguire character in *Jerry Maguire* was largely based on the guy whose number I'm about to dial.

Steinberg was a student at Cal Berkeley—albeit a very unusually accomplished one—when he met quarterback Steve Bartkowski, who was a student living on the dorm floor that Steinberg supervised. This story is Exhibit A in the mythology that is Leigh Steinberg. Anyway, a relationship developed and Steinberg ended up representing Bartkowski, the number-one overall pick in the NFL draft, and negotiating the Atlanta Falcons[1] out of a contract that was, at that time, the richest rookie deal in the history of the league.

Since then, he has represented Troy Aikman, Steve Young, and a truckload of other famous people whose names and reputations precede them. He has represented sixty first-round picks and eight first overall picks. Accounting for merchandising, endorsement deals, signing bonuses, and salaries, an ungodly amount of cash has flowed through this individual. For a sports agent, Steinberg's body of work is astonishing.

He has also had his share of lawsuits and public setbacks and crises that have forced him to, at some level, start over. This alone makes him more interesting than the majority of wealthy, successful people, most of whom just want to bloviate about how the world would be a better place if it had more people like them.

After I say "hello," Steinberg talks nonstop for roughly the next sixty minutes. His first sentence is, "The first thing you need to know is that football players will never be confused with Bolsheviks."

You had me at "Bolsheviks." [2]

Steinberg was, of course, referring to the futility of the NFLPA strike, and explaining that because of how they're wired to think and compete, the players had essentially no chance from the get-go.

"Football players play a sport that has many similarities to the military," he explains. "The culture is rigid. They stand in long lines. They get yelled at. A lot of them are coach's kids who are used to structure. Many of them follow fundamentalist Christianity. They play a violent sport where every play has a great deal of import and could be their last. Maybe most important, they're only paid from September to January, which meant that a lot of those striking players may not have managed their money very well and were stretched pretty thin by the time the strike hit. And then there's the fact that the NFL players had *never* won a strike. There were no older players to reassure the younger players."

In fact, many of the older players turned coaches resented the younger players for striking, creating a massive amount of clubhouse tension across the league. I ask Steinberg about the precarious balancing act that the strike created for a player agent—whose certification, or right to negotiate contracts, was granted (and could subsequently be taken away on a whim) by the NFLPA.

"I came from a union family and was taught never to cross a picket line," he says. "When a player comes off of campus after he's drafted, he has no choice but to sign with that team. It's not like Troy Aikman was going to go back to campus and play cello in the Westwood Philharmonic. Once they're drafted, the team holds all the power and as a player you are stuck with them.

"What they were fighting for was worth fighting for: free agency," he says. "Deciding where you want to live and work based on whatever combination of factors are most important, including money, coaching staff, geography, or a winning team."

It became clear that though free agency was a noble and necessary battleground, the fight wouldn't be won on a picket line. However, the looming strike put agents smack in the middle of the battle.

"Replacement games were opportunities for players to show their skills," he explains. "Quarterback [and replacement quarterback] Kevin Sweeney is my client, and the Cowboys want to sign him to their replacement squad. I'm obligated to act in my client's best interest, and it's in Sweeney's best interest *right now* to take an opportunity to play for the Cowboys. However, the union sent out an advisory stating that agents could be decertified for negotiating for replacements. I had to tell my player I couldn't negotiate his contract."

Money was a very real factor for the striking NFL player in 1987. The rookie minimum was a modest $50,000, prorated by game over a sixteen-game season, and a third-year player making the league minimum brought home only $70,000. Factor in car payments, mortgages, mouths to feed at home, and other expenses, and for many players the financial worry was very real. The idea of the NFL player being "set for life" after signing a contract was largely a misnomer. In 1987 30 percent of all players earned less than $100,000, and 57 percent earned less than $200,000. The average player salary for the Denver Broncos in 1986 was $140,120, which was and is, by any standard, a lot of money. But it's cast in a different light when you realize that the average career span was 4.2 years. Players had a very short window, by and large, in which to make their money.

Another factor working against the union was the fact that free agency may not have been a huge issue to the average, workaday NFL player for whom the "market" for their services may be soft. If teams weren't going to be in a bidding war for a backup tight end, then why strike for an issue that was only going to allow a superstar to pad his bank account? "I don't think free agency is the big issue," said Calvin Magee, a Tampa Bay Buccaneers tight end. "The important issues to me are stuff like the pension plan and severance pay."[3]

Replacement games turned out to be the lever that moved and eventually broke the NFLPA.

"[Regular] players were deeply unsettled and destabilized," says Steinberg. "They like structure. This put a collective emotional depth-charge into player psyches. In the replacement games, the networks used NFL announcing teams, they used NFL graphics, and they had enough interesting names from college football to put a reasonably competitive football product on the field and on television. And for most fans, their knowledge of NFL rosters is not very deep."

The fact that there was a group of players wearing their uniform, in their stadium, in front of their fans, playing on their networks, and sometimes even wearing their jersey was too much for a group (professional football players) already acculturated to paranoia. NFLPA player reps were afraid that their union activity would jeopardize their jobs. It's simplistic to say it, but everybody was against everybody, which is also sort of the deal in football anyway, strike or no.

"When an athlete, no matter what color jersey he wears, finally realizes that opponents and teammates alike are his adversaries, and he must deal and dispense with them all, he is on his way to understanding the spirit that underlies the business of competitive sport," said former Jets receiver George Sauer, on his football ambivalence. "There is no team, no loyalty, no camaraderie; there is only him, alone."[4]

Sauer quit the game at age twenty-seven to write, feeling that pro football had destroyed his sense of values as a human being. To be fair, he was back three years later, catching passes in the upstart World Football League. Football, for all its dehumanizing problems and moral dilemmas, is a hard habit to break, and players realize that there is very little in civilian life that can measure up to the excitement it provides.

For every player there is a fear of the end, particularly of the loss of identity that comes with it. "For thirteen years I lived a fantasy, full of life and dreams come true, emotionally, physically, spiritually," said former Ram defensive end Fred Dryer in *The Thinking Man's Guide to Pro Football*. "You know, of course, that it isn't going to last. There's a part of you, way down deep inside, that's always uneasy about that. And it does end so fast. It all went by in a heartbeat."[5]

"There was a frantic search for information in this period," Steinberg recalls of the three weeks of replacement football in 1987. "I was glued to the phone day and night. Players checked in every day, wondering if I'd heard anything and when it was going to be over. I had rookies who were asking, 'Why did this have to happen in *my* year?' I had veterans who faced the question, 'Should I cross the picket line?'"

Steinberg recalls that the "situation in Kansas City" only escalated the sense of paranoia. The "situation" being that there were regular players driving around in pickup trucks with shotguns and throwing rocks, eggs, and anything else they could get their hands on at the replacements. "It was a wild time. There was a great deal of bitterness."

According to former Chiefs defensive tackle Bill Maas, the "shotgun" story has been blown out of proportion. "About a year before the strike, [Gene] Upshaw would show up at our union meetings and tell us where we were heading, which was toward a strike," Maas recalls. "He'd tell us to save our money, which is like telling a fat kid not to eat cookies."

Upshaw was supposed to be a more conciliatory leader for the NFLPA and improve relations with Jack Donlan, executive director of the NFL Management Council, who had a strained relationship with former union executive director Ed Garvey. "Gene is pro-player; Ed was antimanagement,"[6] said Donlan in a 1987 preseason interview for *Athlon's Pro Football*, June 1987, 199.

"We knew we were going to walk out after the fourth game in 1987 because you need four games to make it an official season," Maas says. "But still, even flying home on the team charter after the fourth game, I remember asking, 'Are we really going on strike? Are we really not showing up for work tomorrow?' And our player rep, Nick Lowery, said 'Yeah, we've gotta show up on the picket line tomorrow.' Well, I went duck hunting that morning with [linebacker] Dino Hackett and [tight end] Paul Coffman, and we drove up in a pickup truck. Coffman said, 'Hey, wanna fire up the guys a little bit?' so we drove over into the Royals' stadium parking lot and he got in the back with a shotgun. Everybody was laughing and it was all a big joke. But that night I turned on CNN and the headline was 'Violence Erupts in Kansas City.'"

* * *

What didn't make sense to Steinberg was the way that on an individual basis and without the benefit of another league for leverage after the USFL folded, he could routinely get larger contracts out of NFL owners. He was beating ownership on an individual basis, but players didn't stand a chance as a collective.

"It created a curious dichotomy," he says. "As a group, the owners were a much more impregnable force. They were completely unified and only spoke through the commissioner."

"We thought we were striking for a better pension and a better severance package," Maas recalls. "Most of us didn't even know what free agency was. We had no idea they were going to bring in scabs because that had never happened before."

However, in some NFL cities, there was covert communication between management and players.

"Lamar Hunt came into town and called me up one night and asked me to come in," says Maas. "He said, 'Can we work this thing out?' So we [Maas and Lowery] went in around 10 p.m. one night. He called up [Commissioner] Pete Rozelle and put him on speakerphone and then eventually called Gene Upshaw, who asked us to go to a separate room."

To the players, the deals that needed to get done were as numerous as the individual players themselves, while the owners essentially had one deal to make. This sent players, agents, and coaches scrambling for a competitive advantage.

"I guarantee you the coaches and management were calling the players," says Steinberg. "It was the ultimate cognitive dissonance. It was simply clear that this was not a strike that was going to be won. Meanwhile, agents felt threatened by the union. Agents would have to go to a yearly conference, and it seemed like there were always loud, angry arguments between the union and agents. There was suspicion that this [union] was a group that wanted to cut agents' fees and eliminate their rights.

"On the other side, the union took it personally whenever any of my clients went against the union. There was anger in every direction. The players were angry at the union, the union was angry at the agents, the agents were angry at the union. Everyone was angry at everyone else."

Among the first three big-name, big-time players to cross were Joe Montana, Howie Long, and Tony Dorsett. While Dorsett was past his prime, the other two were arguably the biggest, most marketable names in pro football in 1987. "Montana's crossing was completely demoralizing to the players," says Steinberg. With their departure, and the replacement games grinding along each week, came the sense that the strike was doomed.

"When the big name guys started crossing the line, it caused a real division in the union," Maas recalls.

Actually, the first big-name player to cross may have been enigmatic Jets defensive end Mark Gastineau, who was as irritating to fellow players as he was talented. "He has an IQ of about room temperature,"[7] said Chicago Bears defensive end Dan Hampton, of his Rolls Royce–driving, fur-coat wearing, and sack-dancing fellow worker. How some of those same qualities—the fur wearing, and Rolls driving—could be charming in one man (like Joe Namath) and irritating in another, is immaterial. What matters is that Gastineau said he felt more loyalty to his owner than to his teammates. "Players have been upset with me before," he said. "There are times when they didn't believe the things I've stood for. It started with the dance. That was something I did out of emotion. They didn't like it."[8]

Gastineau led the league in sacks with nineteen in 1983, and then set an NFL record with twenty-two in 1984, earning him a $4 million contract. "There have been things said about me in the papers by my teammates but never by Mr. Hess," said Gastineau. "He visited me in the hospital last year [after knee surgery]. Those things mean a lot to me."[9]

To Steinberg, however, the important conflict was never primarily about players and management.

"We should have been thinking of this as the NFL vs. Every Other Form of Discretionary Entertainment," he says. "The real battle was to build the brand of pro football, and I was acutely aware of the damage that this was doing to pro football. The most self-destructive thing that could ever happen was withdrawing the product."

The NFL withdrew the product for seven weeks in a 1982 labor dispute, again for a week in 1987, and then replaced it with an alternate product. Much of the 1980s and 1990s were spent regaining the trust of their audience.

"The best result of the strike is that it taught everyone a lesson," says Steinberg. "Never have another cessation of play. The NFL has had continuous play since 1987. Fans know to expect that the season will be played."

7

YOU KEEP ME HANGING ON

John Reaves: First Round to Replacement

I watched *Draft Day* starring Kevin Costner, Denis Leary, and one woman whom I'm sure they added at the eleventh hour because without her it would "just be a bunch of guys talking about football for two hours." As it was, it was still just a bunch of guys and one woman talking about football for two hours.

The NFL's involvement was supposed to make it "realistic" but just made it look like a commercial. This was a two-hour ad for jerseys, season tickets, the NFL Network, the draft itself, Rich Eisen, Chris Berman, and Chevy cars and trucks. It was shot like a commercial, and it looked and sounded like one. I half expected Denis Leary to start a voice-over about foot-pounds of torque while the Costner character drove to the stadium in his brand new Chevy truck. There was nothing artful about it, which is to say that there was nothing that invited the viewer to relate to it on any level. Actually, the most interesting thing about it were the wide shots of the cities—especially Cleveland, which is much cooler than people think and where I spent a great afternoon/ evening going to dinner and prowling record stores a couple of years ago.

Art-wise, this made *The Program* look like *Schindler's List*-meets-*Citizen Kane*. *The Program* was a bad football movie that came out in the mid-1990s, but it's also a bad football movie that I own and watch at least once a year because it's really fun to watch. It's fun because it tries to tackle some issues (e.g., steroids, ethical recruitment) and it has some interesting characters.

The great Sam Elliot had a cameo as a college football coach in *Draft Day*, which created the same discomfort that you would feel if you went to visit your grandfather and, and instead of a sweater and slacks, he greeted you in an Under Armour sweatsuit and a fitted ball cap worn backward.

The NFL will survive the Ray Rice and Adrian Peterson scandals of the 2014–2015 season (if you're unaware of what I mean, simply Google the names "Ray Rice" and "Adrian Peterson"), but it may not survive its own inflated opinion of itself. I recently purchased the entire library of NFL Films "season in review" DVDs and Super Bowl highlight films (thank you, eBay). I was charmed by how, especially in the 1960s and 1970s, the NFL Films crew treated each season like an experimental art film, using unique angles, filters, and music to tell the story of a season. For all its problems (and there were many problems in the 1960s and 1970s, too), football is still a beautiful, interesting game with no shortage of drama and stories.

There's no denying that we live in a lame era where Twitter masquerades as journalism and YouTube masquerades as "television." Everybody is trying so hard to be funny that nobody is actually funny anymore. That said, football should be the thing that is real—real combat between two teams with a scoreboard at the end telling us who is better. My advice to the NFL is this: give us less. Take away Thursdays. Take away the NFL Network. Don't expand to eighteen games. Don't make any more movies. Stop Tweeting. Let the game sell itself.

Former Tampa Bay Buccaneers replacement quarterback John Reaves is aghast over the fact that 33 million people watched the 2014 NFL Draft on television. "Thirty-three *million* people?" he says, guffawing. "Just waiting for *something* to happen!"

His voice is exactly the kind of grizzled, Southern, slightly world-weary voice you would expect to belong to a quarterback who was a first-round draft choice out of Florida in 1972 and didn't play his last professional game until October of 1987. The voice sounds like it should belong to a character in a Dan Jenkins novel and not a real person, and sounds like the kind of voice that might currently be accompanied by a tumbler of scotch and a pack of smokes, though given Reaves's semicheckered background, I take that thought back.[1]

To say that Reaves has been a lot of places and experienced a lot of football, good and bad, would be a colossal understatement. He has been around the proverbial block on a labyrinthine football journey that took him through several NFL franchises in two distinct eras, with more than a dash of USFL thrown in. We share a laugh over the made-for-television drama that is draft day, what with dozens of ESPN or NFL Network talking heads, and nonstop coverage and analysis. We laugh about the soon-to-be millionaires in garish suits in the Green Room at Radio City Music Hall and the bro-hugging that takes place with Commissioner Roger Goodell.

I ask if he remembers how he spent his draft day, in 1972.

"I went down to the offices of the *Gainesville Sun* to watch the AP newswire machine with my friend, Steve Spurrier," he says. "You know the thing that just spits out the paper? Anyway, we're standing there watching this thing, and Spurrier goes, 'Hey, Johnny, this says Philadelphia Eagles select John Reaves.' And that was it.

"I had never talked to anybody from the Eagles or been interviewed by them," he explains, in what is a far cry from the dollars, time, and travel spent evaluating prospective NFL players within an inch of their lives today. It's a far cry from the private jet sent to ferry the newly minted draft choice to team headquarters for a jersey display and press conference photo-op.

"There didn't seem to be a big sense of urgency," he says, when asked if the club reached out to him immediately via phone. "But I do remember that when I played in the Senior Bowl, after one of the practices we were about to get in the shower and the coaches said, 'Make sure you stand around naked for a while after the shower. The scouts are going to come in here and they want to evaluate you.'"

He guffaws at his own story.

*　*　*

Reaves spanned two distinct eras in professional football. His early photographs and football cards are of the decidedly retro, early-1970s variety with a posed photograph on a stock background. He wears a vintage single-bar face mask in the early shots. By 1987, however, most of the league was playing on plastic carpet, some under inflatable domes, while wearing helmets with inflatable inner padding. In 1987, he played on a Tampa Bay Bucs squad with wunderkind rookie quarter-back Vinny Testaverde from Miami, who would go on to play well into the early 2000s.

Reaves played with four teams in nine NFL seasons and had more arrests (three) than victories as a starting quarterback (two). In his rookie season in Philadelphia, he appeared in court on a marijuana charge. Not exactly a sterling way to begin one's pro football career. As a result, Reaves was viewed as damaged goods and bounced around accordingly. This, of course, was in the era of the hard-partying quarter-back—Kenny Stabler, Joe Namath, Dan Pastorini, and so forth—but in the strange moral economy that is professional sports, heavy alcohol use is viewed as "boys will be boysishness," while drug[2] use is cause for concern. Reaves fell into the latter category, and as such, his fond NFL memories were few and far between.

"I got a chance to start for the Bengals against Earl Campbell and the Houston Oilers in the 1975 AFC Wild Card game," he recalls. "My head coach was Paul Brown, and my offensive coordinator was Bill Walsh. It rained seven inches that day, and somehow I got a grip on the ball and threw two TDs. Brown and Walsh gave me the game ball; I still have it."

Much change took place from 1972 to 1987, including a few other strikes, which, according to Reaves, didn't make a significant difference. "The strikes didn't make any change," he explains. "What started the shift toward free agency and bigger money was the USFL. The NFL suddenly had to compete for players."

Reaves made the most of his USFL experience, flourishing in the upstart league for his hometown Tampa Bay Bandits, who in many ways symbolized the way that the USFL combined irreverence with great football. "I had been in the NFL for nine years and hadn't gotten a chance to play much," he recalls. "The USFL gave me an opportunity to play, and I got to play against Steve Young, Doug Flutie, Jim Kelly, Herschel Walker, and all kinds of other great players. On the Bandits we had a bunch of talented receivers like Willie Gillespie and Eric Truvillion, and guys who went on to play well in the NFL like Nate Newton and Gary Anderson."

One of his final USFL games was played in the Los Angeles Memo-rial Coliseum in front of the smallest professional football crowd (4,912 reportedly, although it looked smaller) in the history of that cavernous stadium. The crowd was so small, in fact, that ESPN producers stuck only to tight shots of the field, never letting the cameras wander up to seat level, even on high kicks, an effect that made it look like an early-1980s Saturday morning pro wrestling telecast which, ironically, ESPN was also doing some of in that era.

At any rate, that afternoon Reaves squared off against a struggling USFL rookie named Steve Young, who would, of course, go on to win Super Bowls and enter the Pro Football Hall of Fame, but who at the time was the highest-paid quarterback in pro football history on a team that was on its way to bankruptcy (see nonexistent crowds) and had serious trouble just making payroll. Young was part of a USFL arms race that brought players like Kelly and Flutie, in addition to mid-tier NFL names like Brian Sipe, Chuck Fusina, and Cliff Stoudt to the league, as the USFL tried to outbid the NFL for established talent.

What's interesting about Bandits coach Steve Spurrier's approach is that rather than bidding for an established NFL name (like Sipe) or a college superstar (like Flutie or Young), he basically just gave the quarterbacking job to his friend whose resume over the last decade-plus had been anything but sterling but with whom he (ostensibly) had a comfortable and successful working relationship. What I'm trying to say is that Spurrier in a sense spurned all conventional scouting wisdom and chose relational compatibility and "intangibles" over measurables. As much as we want to make football quasiscientific, like baseball, it's a different and much more relational (and violent) animal in which the presence of twenty-two guys on a field all moving at once makes it hard to get a representative read on anything, scientifically. The fact of the matter is that Spurrier felt comfortable with Reaves as a leader, gambled on him, and ended up being right. This, I feel, would never (or rarely) happen today, what with our astronomical scouting budgets and bevy of "experts," especially as it pertains to projecting quarterbacks.

The other interesting things (to me) about Spurrier in the 1985 ESPN telecast of Bandits/Express is that he coached the game in a loud, multicolored, non-team-logoed, non-officially-licensed golf shirt, prompting Tom Mees to intone, "He's the fashion plate of the USFL." It occurs to me that this (coaches having a modicum of personal style and individuality) won't really happen again. By nature of the logistics of coordinating eleven guys per side, football will always be a mostly

conformist activity, but a large part of me misses the individual flour-
ishes that the USFL accounted for and even celebrated.

Reaves, then thirty-five, was sensational against Young and the Express. Young was struggling coming into the game, with four touchdowns against seven picks, as he was clearly trying to shoulder the
entire offensive burden for his club. In one first-quarter sequence,
Reaves threw a beautiful wheel route to halfback Gary Anderson (who
went on to a distinguished NFL career with San Diego), and then a
sharp comeback to Larry Brodsky before finding Brodsky again on a
deep dig. He finished the game twenty for thirty-eight with a pair of
touchdown throws. It's a game that in the annals of pro football history
will be largely forgotten but that was an interesting example of how the
game changes and ebbs over the years, and an interesting example of
how certain players (like Reaves) can fall through the cracks because
they are perceived as too old or too damaged to get a particular job
done. Quarterbacking, though, is part body, part athletic intelligence,
and part interpersonal acuity.

The Bandits managed to bring fans, around 40,000–45,000 per game
according to Reaves, because they emphasized fun and entertainment.
"They would bury mortgages, and give out million-dollar annuities at
halftime," Reaves says. "And one of our owners was Burt Reynolds."

"Since then, these franchises are worth billions," he says. "And the
players are getting compensated nicely. What does a backup quarterback make in the league now? Half a million dollars? I would have
taken that!"

Instead, in 1972, NFL players operated without agents (for the most
part) and many had day jobs in the off-season. "Average salary was
around $27,000 in 1972," he explains. "We had to work in the off-
season."

❉ ❉ ❉

Reaves was working in Tampa, in commercial real estate, and had been
out of football for two years when he got the call from the Bucs, asking
if he wanted to "give it a try."

"I hadn't played a football game since June 30, 1985, which is the
day they released those hostages," he recalls. "I told them, 'I've been

sitting around for two years,' which wasn't exactly true because I'd been running a little bit."

Reaves played that final game against the USFL's number-one passer, Bobby Hebert, and the Oakland Invaders. The Invaders had a stacked deck of a roster full of future NFL talent, including linebackers Ray Bentley and Gary Plummer, future Pro Bowl wide receiver Anthony Carter, and future Indianapolis Colts running back Albert Bentley[3]

Even given his advanced age, and the fact that he'd already logged thirteen seasons of pro football experience, there is something distinctly boyish and shit-eating about Reaves's publicity-shot grin.[4] It's the grin of a guy who came into the game with twenty-nine interceptions but didn't care. He would go out of the USFL like he came into it—winging the football.

"We think John's ready to play a great one," says Spurrier before the game, from beneath a helmet of 1980s hair. "John's our quarterback." That era's Spurrier was known for play-calling gadgetry and would often start games with onside kicks. On this day, however, he starts with several runs in a row to Gary Anderson, who was the USFL's version of Marshall Faulk, with seventy-two receptions on the season.

He puts together a great three-play sequence late in the first quarter, hitting Anderson over the middle, finding him again on the toughest throw in pro football (the deep out) the following play, and then hitting his tight end Marvin Harvey in the seam. Watching Reaves quarterback in this era is certainly a walk down memory lane, what with routine seven-step drops—a rarity in today's NFL. Incidentally, the Invaders have one of the best color schemes in all of pro football—the light blue accented by thick yellow stripes, with the fist grasping a lightning bolt on the helmet. Very cool. The Bandits' color scheme—silver on white on silver—always just televises as vaguely white from any distance away.

ABC cuts away from the action in the second quarter to report on the release of the TWA hostages, during which Reaves hits Anderson in the end zone to put the Bandits up 14–3. It's not enough of a lead, however, to withstand a Hebert/Carter hot streak in the second half, and though he played well, John Reaves left the field thinking he had played his final pro football game. Until, of course, Perkins and Tampa came calling in 1987.

❋ ❋ ❋

The free-spirited Reaves was soon reminded about the football grind, as delivered by Tampa coach Ray Perkins—he of the Bear Bryant/Alabama old-school coaching tree. "Coach Perkins liked to run us to death," he explains. "He seemed to want to condition the entire team in a day or two."

Reaves's replacement quarterbacking colleague in Tampa, former South Carolina star Mike Hold, remembers it a little differently. "I don't think Perkins was so much trying to get us in shape as we was trying to see who already *was* in shape.

"Fortunately," he laughs, "I was in shape."

Hold was in shape, in part, because of his participation in the inaugural season of the Arena Football League in summer of 1987. The AFL offered a unique brand of football in that it was played with smaller teams, on a smaller fifty-yard field surrounded by padded walls and nets off of which the ball could and did occasionally carom. "Nobody could have projected how popular arena football would become," he says. "Most of us saw it as an opportunity to kill time, keep playing, and stay in shape because most of us had NFL aspirations. When we gathered for a combine at Wheaton College,[5] we knew we only had six weeks to learn a totally different game. We had no idea how it would be perceived by the public."

It was also, frankly, an opportunity to earn money playing football. "I had never really been paid to play up to that point," Hold explains. "We made five hundred bucks a game, plus a one-hundred-and-fifty-dollar win bonus." These modest numbers put Hold's enthusiasm to be a replacement player into some financial context. "I made around nine grand for the strike games, which felt like a whole lot of money to play football."

ESPN held the modest broadcast rights to Arena Football in 1987, and aired Mike Hold's first professional game as a member of the Chicago Bruisers in the Rosemont Horizon.[6] The network went to great lengths to have eccentric former college coach Lee Corso explain the nuances of the rules, even going so far as to have him demonstrate a ball careening off a net. Imagine a super revved-up, little middle-aged man in a sport coat and wingtips running around underneath nets in an empty arena. Surreal and very "1980s." Corso, who had a somewhat mediocre run as a college and USFL head coach, was in 1987 scarcely able to imagine the fixture he would become as, in some ways, a caricature of himself on ESPN's College Gameday program using personality qualities that really made him the perfect guy to help launch the AFL. He was, even then, enthusiastic almost to a frightening degree, and also utterly uncritical.

Hold, who was a little small by NFL standards at 6'0" and 190 pounds, ended up being a perfect fit for the Arena League, where he spent the better part of twenty-three years as a player and a coach. "I miss it," he says. "I miss the AFL. For twenty-three years my resume was arena football. The hard thing is moving around like we did . . . we moved six times in my nine years as a coach." Hold quarterbacked eight different AFL teams from the league's inception through 2000. He was then head coach of the Augusta Stallions (AF2), Carolina Cobras (AFL), and the Macon Knights (AF2).

Hold was working as a graduate assistant coach at South Carolina when his defensive backs coach, Tom McMahon, asked if he was interested in being a replacement player. "He had me call somebody in Tampa," Hold recalls, "and the next thing I know I was on an airplane."

The offensive coordinator in 1987 in Tampa was Marc Trestman, who went on to some renown as a kind of boutique tutor to NFL star quarterbacks and a football eccentric who migrated north to Canada to dominate the CFL in obscurity for a number of years. In the 2014–2015 season, he was head coach of the Chicago Bears and was trying to get something out of Jay Cutler's immense talent. In 1987, he had an arena league quarterback and a thirty-seven-year-old real estate agent in his quarterback room.

"Trestman was analytical and studious like a professor," Reaves explains. "He was a free-agent wide receiver in Minnesota in 1979 when I was with the Vikings. We became friends then, and we threw a lot of passes together."

According to Hold, reception of the replacement players by Bucs veterans varied, but was for the most part low-key. "One time they pulled their cars up to the fence by the practice field and started hooting and hollering," he says. "And then they made sort of a line in the hotel lobby, but a lot of them were stopping us to shake hands and say 'hello' because we'd been together in training camp. It was never a scary or threatening experience for me.

"Tampa was kind of a young team," he recalls. "We had Steve De-Berg, who was probably one of the older and I guess you could say more bitter players. He would make comments about it from time to time afterward, and even though he was kidding, I knew there was some seriousness behind it." DeBerg had logged almost a decade in the league and was with his third team by the time the 1987 strike became a reality. He would play another decade in the league, finally retiring after the 1998 season at age forty-four. He would enjoy his best years as a starter in Kansas City, where he would lead his team to an 11–5 record in 1990, throwing for twenty-three scores and just five interceptions.

Perceived threat or no, the Buccaneers rode in two buses to the Pontiac Silverdome in Detroit on October 4, led by "a snowplow type-thing to break up barricades." According to Hold, there were no barricades, just a few people jeering their arrival, making it not unlike a visiting team's arrival in any NFL city on any average Sunday afternoon.

"Official attendance was 4,919," he says. "For some reason it sticks in my head. It was still loud. I threw two touchdown passes that afternoon . . . and they can't ever take that away. It's in the books. I've got that game film . . . it's something . . . it's cool. I don't ever say 'I played in the NFL,' but still, it's a memory you can't take away. I was still coached by Ray Perkins . . . and I got to go back to camp the next summer and play with guys like Vinny Testaverde and Mike Shula. It was cool."

Both Reaves and Hold, it seems, are grateful for their place in the oddest three weeks in NFL history.

"I understood what the veterans were trying to do, I really did," says Hold. "But I was just a guy looking for an opportunity. We all want to play in the NFL, and at the time there wasn't anybody beating down my door inviting me to a camp. I'm really thankful for it."

"I'm still sneered at by some of the old Bucs," says Reaves. "But I put in my time in the 1974 strike and the 1982 strike . . . and I paid all of my union dues the whole time. It was the chance of a lifetime to get back on the field, and was a wonderful experience. It gave a lot of people the chance to play who were otherwise caught up in the sheer numbers game of the NFL having forty-man rosters. I have no regrets."

8

STAND BY ME

The Regulars: Keith Butler and Jeff Kemp

In 1987, there was perhaps no bigger fan of linebacker and cultural object Brian Bosworth than this author, age eleven. Like The Boz, I had an unfortunate mullety rat-tail with the sides shaved. Like The Boz, I played linebacker. I picked up his "autobiography" entitled *The Boz* (with Rick Reilly)[1] and guffawed aloud at, on one level, what a complete idiot he was at times but also secretly admired how outspoken he had the courage to be in what was still, at that time, a pretty buzzcut, Bear-Bryant-ish, conformity-loving football culture.

The Boz was, in a sense, everything great and also everything distasteful about the 1980s, looking like a jacked-up version of the Iceman character in *Top Gun*. He was refreshingly up front about his desire to make money off of his name and image. He was also refreshingly up front about what a profit-driven meat market college and pro football was and exactly how he planned to cash in at a time when almost nobody was saying these things aloud, even though everybody knew them. It almost worked. He left Oklahoma early, declared for the NFL's amorphous and somewhat mysterious "supplemental draft,"[2] was selected by Seattle (this was the middle of nowhere, from a media perspective, in 1987), and then promptly signed the richest contract in NFL history at the time for roughly $11 million guaranteed over ten years. It was good to be The Boz in 1987.

The Boz rose to prominence during what was, wrote Michael Weinreb, "the height of a period of conspicuous consumption, at a time when we became smitten, as a culture, with power and status and the accumulation of wealth . . . [when] the perpetuation of one's own personal legend, and the generation of dissonant alter egos such as The Boz, and the unprecedented melding of sports and entertainment no longer seemed mutually exclusive from the concept of forming a winning team."[3]

At that time, he was one of the first athletes really using his charisma to sell all manner of products, while also using that same charisma to piss off and annoy a bunch of people in the football and cultural establishment. As a mostly uncool white linebacker from the Midwest, I loved him because, facing facts, it was no secret that everybody cool in sports at that time was black.

He was also, allegedly, an early adopter in the burgeoning pro-sports steroid culture, which probably contributed both to his ascension and his downfall. On an informal steroid-and-marketable-stars timeline, he would be followed very closely by guys like Jose Canseco and Mark McGwire, who parlayed comic-book bodies and on-field production into big dollars and temporary notice in the mainstream public's consciousness.

It's a little awkward, then, when I mention Brian Bosworth to Keith Butler. "Boz replaced me on the Seahawks," he says, nonchalantly. "It was my last season . . . I mean, I didn't know it was my last season." Butler was the anti-Boz[4] in many ways—rock solid, steady, and professional. "Brian was a good guy," he recalls. "He just wanted to be a regular guy around the team. But Brian had some natural flaws in his game that were exposed by the NFL . . . and the NFL always exposes those flaws. He had small hands and small feet. He hurt his shoulders . . . " This is a kind way of saying that perhaps Bosworth's frame wasn't equipped for the amount of muscle and bodyweight it was being asked (by the steroids) to carry.

Butler would know, having served the Pittsburgh Steelers as a linebackers coach for the last decade[5] and helping to build some of the most successful team defenses in NFL history with coordinator Dick LeBeau. It is in this capacity that Butler has shaped the careers of NFL superstars like James Harrison, LaMaar Woodley, and James Farrior, but has also had a close look at the fruits of his generation's labor dispute. Simply stated, today's NFL player makes a ton of money and doesn't always handle the money (or the attendant pressure) correctly. Bosworth, in some ways, was a bygone era's version of today's player.

"Money today has changed the perspective of the player," Butler explains. "Some can handle it, and some can't. With that kind of money on the table you have to have production. One of our guys, LaMaar Woodley, was hurt last season and saw his numbers and sacks go down through no fault of his own. But I always tell guys, 'They're not gonna pay you to stand on the sidelines with me.'"

In 1987, the Seahawks were led by head coach Chuck Knox, who was stern, old school, and from a decidedly union perspective, having grown up near Pittsburgh. He had already served in head coaching stints with the Los Angeles Rams and Buffalo Bills. And it was his job to coach the replacement players as mandated by ownership.

"It was a touchy situation for the coaches," says Butler. "They had to do what they had to do. I talked to [longtime Steelers defensive coordinator] Dick LeBeau about it, who was coaching in Cincinnati at the time, and he had a lot of replacement players who had no idea about very basic defensive concepts. Some of the guys were two or three years [or more] out of football. Some were late training camp cuts, some were early cuts and some were right off the street."

"As players we talked about it a lot and knew it was coming," he recalls. "I had gone through a strike in 1982. We wanted to move toward free agency, and some of us believed in what we were trying to get accomplished. We thought it was important for players to get a chunk of the huge money that the NFL was generating."

The players would eventually see that chunk and would eventually see free agency, but Butler knew, by and large, he wouldn't be around to enjoy any of the fruits of the strike.

"What was sad was that the owners made sure the players had to stay out a third game," he says, alluding to the fact that the dispute was technically settled *before* the third strike game on October 18. "I ended up losing money I never made up again. All told, I think I lost $80,000 during the strike."

Some of Butler's teammates—including superstar Steve Largent—crossed the line, creating a touchy clubhouse dynamic in Seattle.

Wrote Bosworth in *The Boz*, "I didn't respect guys like our kicker, Norm Johnson, whom we now call 'Scab.' He crossed. So did Freddie

Young. My gut feeling was we should win as a team and stay out as a team. I lost total respect for the players who crossed. Steve Largent crossed, too, but he has a kid with cerebral palsy and his doctor bills were outrageous. But those other guys, like our quarterback Jeff Kemp, had no balls."[6]

Jeff Kemp, who I spoke with via phone, remembers it differently. "My dad was from Buffalo, which was a union town," he recalls. "In one sense, pro football was the same as Lackawanna Steel. But he also understood owners and understood business, and I was raised with his free-market mind-set. For me, in 1987, I was in my first year with Seattle and I had a contract that I was comfortable with. Steve Largent and I talked about the strike issue a lot as Christians. We prayed about it with our wives. And ultimately, we both felt that we needed to be faithful to the contracts we signed."

"It was tense," Butler remembers. "There were almost a couple of fights. A very good friend of mine, Steve Largent, crossed the picket line. Jacob Green got in his face and there were hard feelings . . . it takes a while to heal. Ultimately, the guys who were striking didn't want the nonstrikers to enjoy the benefits of the strike."

Green also apparently spent some time in Bosworth's face over the matter. "We almost exchanged fist sandwiches over it,"[7] wrote Bosworth, who explained that instead of being a newly minted $11 million athlete marching with a sign on a picket line, he instead chose to go to New York to appear on MTV with "Downtown" Julie Brown,[8] which (the decision to do so) raised the ire of his teammates. "We were a divided team," wrote Bosworth of the end of the strike. "Half of the guys were still pissed about the strike. The other half were pissed off at the guys who crossed the line."[9]

Kemp recalls a heated meeting at teammate Mike Tice's deli. "The arguments rose in tone as a few guys had a few more beers," he says. "I feel like most of the guys wanted to go back and play by the third week of the strike. But the longer we stayed there, the more the 'screw the owners!' mentality took over. It became an 'us against them' dynamic, and I've never been a big 'us against them' type of guy. Ultimately, the tide turned. A few of us decided to go back in and play. Unfortunately, it wasn't a bonding experience."

* * *

I am somewhat sheepish when I admit to my game DVD provider that the strike games are a bit of a holy grail, though he doesn't judge. As collectors, our motives are all mixed and convoluted and intensely personal/nostalgic. For me, there is a strange aesthetic comfort in viewing the old stadiums, the old graphics, the old jerseys (which have sleeves), the old strategies, old coaches with actual distinct personalities and aesthetics,[10] the lack of fantasy football content,[11] grass fields the quality of which varied by groundskeeper, and even the old AstroTurf. If I had as extensive a collection as my contact, I daresay that I would rarely turn on the television on Saturday or Sunday afternoons anymore. Today's spandex-driven, sleeveless jerseys look like sausage casings, in my opinion. Nobody really wants to see a 350-pound offensive guard in a body-hugging spandex onesie. Give me sleeves and non-ridiculous-looking helmets any day. I miss traditional fullbacks and the I-formation. And regarding coaching personalities, name a current coach, besides Rex Ryan, whom you'd actually want to talk or listen to. It's hard to do. Maybe Pete Carroll and Chip Kelly, but it's a short list.

This rootedness in and fascination with the past must come from someplace. There must be something happening on a psychological level that draws me to this era and these players. I think, at some level, it's the earnestness of the era. There was something in the straightforwardness and snark-free[12] presentation of the games that gave us license to care and dream about it. Even the Topps football cards from that era are charmingly straightforward and folksy. In 1987, there weren't foil packs, holographic cards, or cards with pieces of players' jerseys clipped and embedded. They featured simple photos of the player on the front, with "personal data" on the back, such as "Fred Smerlas enjoys weightlifting and camping."

There were, for the most part, no sideline reporters in 1987, and as such there were none of the awkward on-field interviews with coaches like there are now, in which the annoyed-and-interrupted-looking coach says something unique and insightful like, "We need to not turn the ball over." There was no fantasy football, so there was no ticker running along the bottom part of the screen with real-time updates on the players' statistical output.

Maybe it's simply that we all want to go back and relive certain, simpler parts of our lives in which football played a more significant role in our happiness, a time when our minds and hearts were uncluttered to the degree that the games could really matter to us.

❀ ❀ ❀

The Pontiac Silverdome, a once-great stadium situated in a once-good suburb on the north side of Detroit, is now a haunted, bombed-out relic on par with the kinds of haunted and bombed-out relics that have been photographed so artfully by hipster types who are interested in archiving the dissolution of an American city. Stated more simply, the Silverdome is a hot mess. Seeing the interior is like being inside one of those little cameras that are used to show the *Titanic* wreckage. Entire Silverdome rooms and bars look to have been abandoned as is, with champagne glasses waiting on a table to be filled or catering chafing dishes ready to be filled with whatever the reporters are being served on a Sunday afternoon. Other rooms are completely trashed. It's Chernobylian in its state of both disrepair and "someone just up and left" hauntedness.

The fabric roof, which was en vogue in the 1980s, is now in tatters, leaving the trademark Honolulu-blue seats exposed to all manner of snow, ice, birds, and other skyborne Detroit-area debris. The old-style AstroTurf field is still down but has been hopelessly waterlogged and uncared for. It also is littered with debris—namely, parts of the aforementioned fabric roof. An entrepreneur bought the place for a little over a half a million dollars a few years ago, hoping to revive it as a venue for tractor pulls, concerts, and the like, though the idea has devolved to the point that current ownership is just selling off individual seats and toilets (gah) at auction to interested fans.

As Silverdome tenants, the Detroit Lions never advanced to a Super Bowl and barely sniffed the playoffs. Their brightest singular achievement during the Silverdome years was the drafting of Barry Sanders, who brought joy to Lions fans in spite of his team's general and long-standing ineptitude. And although the Lions never advanced to a title game, the stadium was home to the USFL-champion Michigan Panthers. The Panthers had Bobby Hebert, Ray Bentley, and Anthony Carter, who all went on to productive NFL careers, as well as the best linebacker you've never heard of, a rangy outside linebacker named John Corker who, were it not for a drug problem, may well have gone on to dominate the NFL in much the same way as ex-USFLers Sam Mills and Reggie White.

Star Seattle wide receiver Steve Largent crossed the picket line in just enough time to suit up for Seattle's visit to the Pontiac Silverdome to face the Detroit Lions on October 18, 1987—the final weekend of strike football. The regular players had all agreed, in principle, to return to action the following week, and there was an air of anticipation for that event, as networks ran "the real players are back next week!"–type promos.

In 1987, the building was magnificently inflated and bright, though the panning camera revealed an abundance of empty seats. Quarterback Jeff Kemp and center Blair Bush would join Largent as Seahawk offensive regulars, and defensive standout Fredd Young crossed the line as well. The Lions are aided by the return of defensive end William Gay. There is a high school cheerleading squad on the sideline, adding to the surreal, hollow-sounding interior of the dome, giving it the auditory sensation of watching a high school state championship game. Also, as is customary of most games in the dome-and-old-AstroTurf era, the picture is eerily clean, crisp, and precise. I can see why the TV brass fought hard for the old turf, even though it decimated the bodies of the players. It photographs nicely.

Stan "Father of Braylon" Edwards is Detroit's starting running back, appearing after a standout career at the University of Michigan and a journeyman career in the NFL prior to 1987. He's joined by Todd Hons, who played for Lions coach Darryl Rodgers at Arizona State, and former USFL star Eric Truvillion at wide receiver. On the first play from scrimmage, Detroit replacement center Chuck Steele is injured, giving analyst Jimmy Cefalo time to explain that he had played previously in a league in Finland.

On Seattle's first series, Kemp[13] (a roster backup) quickly hits Largent over the middle. Largent's catch reminds me of the sublime non-uniformity of NFL uniforms in the 1980s. In 1987, NFL teams weren't tied to a single uniform provider as they are today, with Nike outfitting the whole of the NFL such that even though the color schemes are different the jerseys all sort of have the same spandex-y, overly accented look. In the mid- to late 1980s, the Seahawks were distinctive because of the fact that their jerseys had large porthole mesh underneath the shoulder panels, giving them a distinctly collegiate look. They also had oversized numbers on the front, back, and shoulders. NFL teams used a variety of jersey manufacturers in the 1980s. In fact, the Cleveland Browns and Pittsburgh Steelers were still using jerseys made of the old Durene fabric that was popularized in the 1960s but had mostly fallen out of fashion in favor of mesh designs by the late 1970s.

Also, somewhat inexplicable given that they played at least nine of their games per annum on AstroTurf, certain Seahawk jerseys from this era always appeared dirty or "off-white."

On the very next play, Largent runs a seam route into the end zone and the Seahawks go up by a touchdown.

"Everything Steve ran got open," Kemp recalls. "It was a fun atmosphere in the huddle because some of the players were in awe of Largent." Kemp would experience a strained relationship for the rest of the season with his striking Seahawk teammates. "Our union rep on defense was our great safety Kenny Easley," he says. "Some of the guys on defense really didn't talk to me for the rest of the season. But it was different with Steve . . . they weren't as upset with him because he had earned their respect by playing so well for so many years."

What's interesting to note about Largent's performance in this game is that, compared to the replacement players he's up against, he's probably still at a distinct physical disadvantage being that he's a relatively small white guy without any particularly noteworthy physical attributes. Still, Largent differentiates himself and puts on a bit of a clinic because of what he knows about route running, body position, and what scouts today call "separation," which can really just be called "the ability to get open." In fact, there's nothing special at all about the route except that he throws the niftiest of shoulder fakes at the line of scrimmage and then just darts up the seam.

The Silverdome always looked positively cavernous, but it looks especially cavernous with nobody in it, as is the case for this game. Early in the first quarter the telecast mysteriously cuts to a black screen for several minutes, over which you can still hear Cefalo and Charlie Jones reporting the action and opining as per usual. The picture returns in time to see Hons throw his second interception. A play later, Kemp finds Largent in single coverage (again) in the slot (again) and he throws the exact same route at the exact same spot on the field on which they scored a few minutes earlier. Largent has his second touchdown before Detroit has even remotely considered crossing the fifty-yard line. It is

Largent's eighty-ninth career touchdown, moving him ahead of Don Maynard and into second all-time in league history.

Detroit's next series is composed of three Gary Ellerson runs and then a punt, communicating their level of confidence in one Todd Hons. Largent strikes (pun intended, sort of) again on the following series, catching a simple slant and taking it fifty-six yards on a nifty run-after-catch. The Detroit corner charged with defending him, Maurice Harvey, looks as though he would rather be anywhere else doing anything else. Harvey has seven NFL seasons under his belt but looks severely overmatched here. Largent switches sides later in the drive and begins to destroy the other corner, John Bostic. Before the first quarter is even close to finished, he has already collected 5 passes for 114 yards.

He catches his third touchdown a few plays later on a pick play to the corner, which is, from a Detroit perspective, really nobody's fault because Seattle executed the play perfectly.

Offensively, Detroit's philosophy appears to be "run as many dives to Gary Ellerson as is humanly possible so as to keep the clock running." It's not a bad strategy save for the fact that they're behind by three touchdowns, and it's still the first quarter. Stan Edwards appears on the stat sheet late in the first quarter on a fake-dive-bootleg for Detroit's second first down.

The highlight of the first half comes on a hit delivered by Fredd Young to Ellerson. Ellerson takes a handoff off-tackle and darts upfield, unaware of the unblocked and quickly pursuing Young, who in perfect form-tackling fashion gets his head in front and uncoils on Ellerson, sending him flying. For those who appreciate linebacking and defense, it is a thing of beauty. This is one of the few replacement games in which the regulars (Kemp, Young, Largent) seem to be playing at a level that transcends everyone else on the field. It could be that they've had two weeks of rest.

Charlie Jones makes an insightful statement when he explains that "replacement football is like the second half of preseason games" in that they feature players who would most likely be cut in camp but who are still very good. Both teams are playing a very vanilla, almost blitzless, 3-4 defense. You can almost tell which replacement ball coaches are into it and which are not. Darryl Rodgers looks like he's in line at the DMV.

Kemp fumbles a shotgun snap deep in his own territory early in the second quarter, giving Detroit its first real sign of life. The ball is recovered by a linebacker named Carl Carr who is, according to the graphic, a car salesman (which is nomenclaturally interesting, if not significant) and the holder of a degree in studio art. Detroit scores on the following play, on a fade from Todd Hons to Danny Bradley. It's a hard throw, and Hons executes it perfectly. Bradley is a former option quarterback at the University of Oklahoma.

On the ensuing series, Largent catches two passes in a row and continues to have his way with the Detroit secondary. By the middle of the second quarter, he's already had a career day, with 8 catches for 145 yards and 3 scores. Kemp's scoring strike to Jimmy Teal to end the drive is significant only because it doesn't go to Steve Largent.

It's worth noting that Largent had an escalator clause in his contract (as many players did and do) in which if he caught greater than sixty balls in 1987, he would receive an additional $100,000 in bonus money. So his destruction of the Detroit secondary had major financial implications as well. He only had four receptions on the season coming into the game.

Aside: Not to dwell too heavily on coach fashion, but Chuck Knox wore a Mr. Rogers-esque gray cardigan sweater with his bright blue "Seattle Seahawks" trucker-style cap being his only piece of team-affiliated adornment. He looked slightly more engaged in the proceedings than Rodgers (Darryl, not Mr.) but not much so.

Rodgers said, of the awkward mixing of replacement players with regulars at the end of the strike, "It's like taking two dates to the prom and hoping they don't meet." In fact, Detroit's "A" team practiced on Saturday in the Silverdome, shortly before their replacement team. They used separate locker facilities.

Largent breaks his own personal bests near the end of the half, with twelve catches for more than 200 yards and the three scores. Contextually, he is near the NFL record for receptions per game, held by Tom Fears with eighteen, though the idea of breaking actual NFL records in replacement games is probably distasteful for everyone involved.

※ ※ ※

Elsewhere around the league, Doug Flutie was making his Patriots debut after a trade from Chicago, and the Three Rivers Stadium sellout streak in Pittsburgh was broken after 119 games. On the last day of strike football, many veteran players lined up alongside remaining replacement players.

"Some of these [replacement] players have trouble with the basics, like catching the ball," deadpans former Vikings receiver Ahmad Rashad at halftime. "They fumble a lot," adds former Bills linebacker Paul McGuire.

* * *

Another unique feature of NFL football in 1987 was the presence of the "Budweiser kickoff," which was a red, graphical frame in the middle of which was the kicking team's kicker. It's an interesting example of (and foreshadowing of) the kind of sponsor-everything ethos that pervades sports today as logos and advertisements creep into nearly every aspect of the game but also an example of how in 1987 the NFL wasn't all that concerned about its image vis-à-vis drinking, meaning that they didn't necessarily care that Little Johnny watching the game at home would potentially forever equate Seahawks kicker Norm Johnson with the unmistakable red-and-white logo adorning a crisp, cool Budweiser.

Oddly, Largent starts the second half on the sideline but quickly returns to catch his thirteenth ball (243 yards) in (intentional or unintentional) pursuit of Fears's record, as well as the single-game yardage record held by Stephone Paige. Why Seattle continues to throw the ball almost exclusively is anybody's guess. After his fourteenth catch, he appears to want to fight most of the Detroit secondary. After Largent's fifteenth catch, almost another touchdown, Charlie Jones explains that Detroit corner Maurice Harvey is going to "have burn marks all over him."

Largent ends his day with 15 catches, 261 yards, and 3 touchdowns—all Largent and Seahawk records. He is shown resting and chatting on the sideline in the third quarter, his day over, and eventually Jeff Kemp gives way to backup Bruce Mathison, who had originally intended to be the Houston Oilers replacement quarterback, until he traveled to Houston to be met by veterans who were "throwing rocks and eggs and stuff." Seeking an environment that was a little more "stable," he ended up in Seattle, where he had a successful run as the Seahawks' replacement quarterback before Kemp's return.

Mathison was a backup in college at the University of Nebraska. He had the distinction of being a traditional dropback pocket passer at a school that was famous in the 1980s for running the option and thereby throwing the ball around four times a game. Still, he had a skill set that was intriguing enough that the San Diego Chargers used a late-round draft choice on him, and he had several cups of coffee as an NFL backup (San Diego, Buffalo) in addition to his run during the strike. Actually, Mathison is an interesting example of my "looks the part" theory of NFL scouting, particularly at the quarterback position. Mathison was the right height (6'3") and had the sort of blond, square-jawed comic-book-hero looks valued by NFL clubs at that position in that era. Simply stated, he probably looked more like an NFL quarterback than played like one.

Whatever electricity there was in the building is officially gone once Largent removes his helmet for the last time. The game ends with Seattle on top 37–14. Official attendance is 8,310, or roughly 10 percent of the cavernous dome.

"I don't like it when unions insult replacement workers and call them 'scabs,'" Kemp explains. "They are just guys looking for an opportunity and trying to provide for their families. I was totally opposed to that, and it rubbed me the wrong way. I was a free agent and fought my way into the league against 50:1 odds. I wasn't going to call anyone a scab."

Finally, I ask Kemp if he was surprised that the owners actually put replacement players on the field.

"I don't think I was shocked," he says. "We called their bluff, and they called ours."

9

THE LAST EMPEROR
Montana

Bill Walsh called it "The Replacement Bowl." The San Francisco 49ers would host Gene Stallings and the St. Louis Cardinals in Candlestick Park to bring an end to strike football. They would do so with Joe Montana and Dwight Clark in uniform, along with several other notable 49er regulars, including tight end Russ Francis and running back Roger Craig.

Montana's impact on the league, and on the strike, is unmistakable. In 1987, he was the de facto emperor of the quarterback position, piloting a 49er dynasty that became known as the "team of the 1980s." There were precious few challengers to his throne. Dan Marino hadn't won a title (and wouldn't), Jim Kelly hadn't yet fully hit his stride in Buffalo, Jim McMahon couldn't stay healthy in Chicago, and John Elway wouldn't win until the 1990s, when a running game arrived in Denver in the person of Terrell Davis.

Relationships between players and ownership were believed to be especially chummy in San Francisco, due in large part to owner Eddie DeBartolo's willingness to take first-rate care of his players. And nowhere was that relationship warmer than between owner and quarterback, as DeBartolo was known to socialize with his star off the field. This, no doubt, created a measure of conflict in Montana, who, though he was raised in union-centric Pennsylvania steel country, didn't strike with the players' union in 1982.

The year 1987 was Montana's ninth year in the league, and the slight-framed quarterback had already racked up his share of injuries and taken his share of punishment, already guiding his club through what seemed like multiple eras and multiple personnel changes. There was far from a sense of finality for Montana in 1987, but there was a sense that he was a player with a shelf life. The acquisition of prospect Steve Young, who had already been through semidebacles in the USFL and Tampa Bay, only underscored Montana's sense of football mortality.

Montana crossed the picket line during the second week of strike football and led the 49ers to victory over Atlanta. On a sunny afternoon in Candlestick Park, he is joined in the backfield by rookie Doug DuBose and burgeoning superstar Roger Craig. He immediately finds tight end Russ Francis on a crossing route for a first down, working behind what was primarily a replacement offensive line with the exception of two marginal regulars.

He then hits Craig on a screen, and the Nebraska tailback seems to be moving at a different, faster, speed than the rest of the players on the field.

"They look just like the normal 49er team," says analyst Ken Stabler.

However, there is an out-of-sync quality to Montana's offense, as he is whistled for a delay-of-game deep into the opening drive. The penalty doesn't cause head coach Bill Walsh to deviate from his script, which was a list of twenty to twenty-five play calls that wouldn't change regardless of down and distance, penalties, and so forth. The script was one of many Walsh innovations that ostensibly took some of the guesswork out of play calling and could serve to calm down his quarterback early in the game. Today, many teams script their opening series or two.

After a St. Louis stop, a replacement punter named Jim Asmus takes the field, prompting Jim Lampley to intone, "Bill Walsh describes Asmus as only an average punter." While on one hand it must have been a thrill to be "described" by Bill Walsh at all, I'm sure this wasn't the endorsement Asmus was looking for.

There has perhaps never been a starting quarterback disparity this extreme in league history, as St. Louis starts a replacement named Sammy Garza, who played collegiately at the University of Texas at El Paso (UTEP) and would make his first pro start at age twenty-two. He would face 49er regulars at defensive end, in Pete Kugler and Dwaine

Board, and would do so behind a patchwork replacement offensive line. Garza starts in place of former Boston College standout Shawn Halloran, also a replacement.

"The experience was awesome," Halloran recalls. "I didn't get much of a chance to play during camp, and the strike gave me a chance to play and get noticed." Sensing a looming strike, the Cardinals organization offered Halloran a $1,000 "contract" when he was cut, essentially obligating him to the club in the event of a strike. "Only during game day when the busses crossed the picket lines was it tough," he recalls. "After the strike was over, the veteran players apologized for their actions. My relationships were with [regular quarterbacks] Neil Lomax and Cliff Stoudt. Both players were understanding of my actions to cross and play and apologized for anything they said or did that might have bothered me."

The 49ers would lead the league in both offense and defense in 1987 and would do so despite their reputation as a "finesse team." They would also compile the best record in the NFL.

Montana had already won two Super Bowl MVP honors by 1987, came back dramatically from injury in 1986, and had already thrown for over 22,000 yards and 147 touchdowns. Yet he still, for some reason, couldn't quite escape the feeling that the 49ers were always planning a little bit too hard for the day he wouldn't be there anymore.

He sails an interception to regular Cardinals safety Travis Curtis near the end of the second quarter that gives life to a St. Louis offense powered by rookie tailback Derrick McAdoo, who has already amassed fifty-one rushing yards and a score. McAdoo, from Baylor, is the nephew of former NBA star Bob McAdoo. He runs violently, and his enthusiasm is evident. The Cardinals offense is as simple as it can be for Garza, who is often handing the ball off to McAdoo on lead plays behind fullback Earl Ferrell. He scores his second touchdown of the day on a nifty little college-style option pitch from Garza.

"He's playing for a job," says Stabler.

With two minutes remaining, Montana then executes the kind of surgical drive that made him famous, culminating in a touchdown pass to Dwight Clark, to pull to within a touchdown, at 21–14.

Halftime features two awesome things—one, a Tegrin dandruff shampoo advertisement featuring a predisgrace Pete Rose and an 1980s-hot woman running her hands through Rose's helmet of hair.

The other, more significantly, is an interview featuring striking quarterbacks Jim Kelly and Ken O'Brien. Announcer Brent Musburger surreally references a drinking game in which the striking O'Brien would drink a beer every time strike-breaker Mark Gastineau would record a sack.

"I don't think there will be any dirty shots against Mark," says striking tackle Mark May. "We're all professionals."

"It's a hard game to watch," says Bills quarterback Jim Kelly of the replacement Bills' tilt with the Giants. "It's a 0–0 tie. The fans are on the edge of their seats."

"We had more than our share of problems because we had a lot of veterans cross the picket line," says O'Brien. "There's no doubt there are hard feelings that are going to last a long time . . . I think there are so many guys who are pro-union . . . it's going to be hard to contain their emotions."

Jim Kelly lost close to $300,000 by striking. "My father was a union rep," says Kelly. "My family is behind me; definitely the players." He then alludes to the fact that some of the striking Bills veterans would be unwilling to block for a Bills fullback who crossed the picket line.

May explains that the Washington Redskins are one of the only teams to completely stay together as a striking unit. None of their veterans crossed the line, yet they were undefeated in replacement games. Their unity would serve them well during a Super Bowl run later in the season.

"The thing that hurt the union more than anything was that solidarity was broken by guys crossing the line," says O'Brien.

The 49ers get an interception from Dana McLemore to start the second half. McLemore was a former regular and former starter in San Francisco, cut in 1986. Strike football represented a chance for him to rekindle his career. And then Joe Montana does what he so often does, which is using Dwight Clark, Roger Craig, and Russ Francis to move the football down the field. On a third and five, the Cardinals come out in a nickel formation (five defensive backs) and the Niners come out in a run-heavy formation, but Montana simply takes a three-step drop and throws a six-yard hitch to Clark. It's like stealing, because, inexplicably, cornerback Mark Jackson is giving Clark a ten-yard cushion. Roger Craig powers the ball in from the one to tie the score at 21–21.[1]

On the ensuing series, Derrick McAdoo goes down after a routine carry. He would leave the game, but his story would have a redemptive ending, as he stuck with St. Louis after the strike and played in nine games in 1988. Sammy Garza's lone pass-game threat, regular wideout J. T. Smith, would come up hobbling as well.

For what it's worth, the old Cardinals uniform, with an unfierce-looking bird head on a simple white helmet, black and red numbers and stripes on white jerseys and pants, is one of the sharpest-looking uniforms in NFL history. Their "new" uniform concept, complete with a fiercer-looking bird and multiple jersey panels, as is the rage, looks like something out of the Mid-American Conference.

McAdoo returns to convert a fourth and one and then a few plays later slashes for twelve more yards to go over 100 for the game to go with a pair of touchdowns. St. Louis is doing it all on the ground, evincing a total lack of faith in Sammy Garza. Garza attempts two quarterback sneaks from the one-yard line and is stoned both times. On fourth and one, McAdoo pushes the ball over on a controversial call, meaning that the only person in Candlestick Park who thought he scored was the line judge who made the call.

Montana quickly strikes back, hitting Roger Craig with a pass over the middle, which he takes to the house, weaving through a replacement Cardinals defense. The score is knotted at 28–28 with twelve minutes to go. "We're going to find out about a young man named Sammy Garza in the final twelve minutes," says Jim Lampley.

Lampley and Stabler bloviate over one of the best football hits I've ever seen on a Doug Dubose sweep, in which he absolutely trucks the cornerback who has come up in run support. The loud crack reverberates through the stadium. Dubose then gets up and glowers over the fallen defensive back (who also, eventually, gets up). It's a great football moment.

Montana eventually passes San Francisco to a 34–28 victory. The 49ers went 3–0 in replacement football, though that record should be asterisked by the fact that many of their regulars played in those games. "It's been a dismal three weeks for the fans," says Lampley, "though replacement football has not been without its entertainment value."

10

WITH OR WITHOUT YOU

Adrian Breen and the End of Strike Football

One of my particular and strange football fetishes is centered around the idea of a dominant running game. That is, a team that primarily runs; runs powerfully and controls the football, the clock, and consequently the game. Let's be clear—neither the replacement Bengals nor replacement Browns had this, but in their first two weeks of replacement football, the hastily assembled Bengals had run for 489 yards and passed for only 47. Their game with Cleveland to end strike football would be an interesting study, if nothing else.

On paper, this was a mismatch of epic proportions, as Cleveland returned regulars, including quarterback Gary Danielson, wideout Brian Brennan, future Hall of Fame tight end Ozzie Newsome, and defensive ends Sam Clancy[1] and Carl Hairston. The only Bengals to cross were linebacker Reggie Williams and defensive end Eddie Edwards.

NFL front office legend Ernie Accorsi was with the Cleveland Browns during the 1987 strike and said in *The GM*, "Before we left [for Cincinnati] I got a phone call from Gary Danielson—he was the veteran quarterback behind Bernie Kosar—and Gary wanted to meet at Art Modell's house. He brought along Ozzie Newsome, the tight end, and Brian Brennan, the receiver, and Rickey Bolden, the left tackle. 'We're all older guys,' Gary said. 'I'm thirty-nine, okay? Let Bernie and the younger guys stay out to avoid recriminations. But if a handful of veterans at just the right positions crossed the picket line, we should be able to steal this game.'"[2]

The replacement Bengals obsession with running the football is all the more curious given the pedigree of Bengals head coach Sam Wyche, then in his fourth season. Wyche was an assistant under pass-game guru Bill Walsh and was known around the league as an emerging offensive force, if not yet a genius like his mentor.

"I always felt like Sam Wyche's heart just wasn't in it," explains Bengals replacement quarterback Adrian Breen of his head coach's approach to the strike games. "To me, it was obvious in how he handled us and his game planning and play calling. I believe our sixty-one rushing attempts in Seattle stands as a franchise record. But in my opinion, most of the position coaches were very engaged."

Breen explains that even Wyche's methods of relaying the plays to his replacement quarterbacks was a little unorthodox, given the short time they had to work together. "San Diego came to town for the first replacement game, and the day before, at the walk-through, Sam says, 'How are we gonna get the plays in?' I assumed we would use a messenger guard or wide receiver to run them in. Sam said, 'Meet me at Union Terminal in Cincinnati,' and we met for a couple of hours to go over a system of hand signals. I think [Bengals replacement quarterback] Dave Walter and I stayed up until three in the morning going over those calls."

"Sam would put us in practice and say you have to complete 70 percent of your passes in practice before I call them in the game," Breen recalls. "It seems like we'd complete 90 percent, and he still wouldn't call them. It's strange, because in [training] camp we were drinking from the firehose, in terms of having the entire playbook thrown at us—with multiple formations, motions, and everything. But once the strike games started, it seemed like we were running the same ten plays."

Football being the intensely relational experience it is, it makes sense that strike football was as tough on the coaches as it was on the striking players. NFL coaching staffs had spent months and sometimes years cultivating relationships with their regular roster players—learning their hot buttons, learning styles, family issues, and inside jokes. For three weeks all of that interpersonal history was gone, replaced by brand new faces and bodies, with the understanding that there was little value in investing long term in the replacement players as the strike could be over at any moment. In this context, Wyche's odd behavior makes sense.

Tension was high between Bengals regulars and replacements, and in fact, the regular players assembled outside the locker room before game time, demanding to play. Breen and his replacement teammates figured their time was up, but Bengals owner Paul Brown had other ideas.

"Paul Brown came into the locker room and said to us, 'You're my Cincinnati Bengals. You went to bat for me, now I'm going to bat for you," Breen recalls. "We were sky high. Fired up."

Across the field, Browns quarterback Gary Danielson would throw his first competitive, regular-season pass since 1985. The former Purdue standout had enjoyed a few seasons as a starter in Detroit but seemed more suited to the backup role into which he had settled comfortably in Cleveland. He would enjoy the luxury of throwing to Brennan and Newsome, while the entire Bengals offense was comprised of replacements—most of whom would be out of pro football by the end of the weekend.

Danielson enters the game with an even seventy-seven touchdowns and seventy-seven interceptions on his career, noteworthy perhaps because it just speaks to the sheer amount of pro football he's played. He gets off to a rough start, however, fumbling an exchange from replacement center Mike Katolin.

It doesn't take Danielson long, however, to settle into a rhythm with veteran receiver Brian Brennan. Brennan seems able to get open at will and doesn't waste any time shredding the Bengals secondary. Not flashy, Brennan nonetheless led the Browns with fifty-five receptions in 1986. Cleveland also does its share of pounding between the tackles— regular All-Pro Cody Risien and regular Rickey Bolden[3]—out of a simple I-formation.

Ironic, then, that Danielson caps Cleveland's first scoring drive on perhaps the most popular current offensive play concept—a bubble screen to Brennan, in which Brennan takes a couple of steps back from the line of scrimmage at the snap, collects the pass, and then charges for the goal line behind a convoy of blockers. The play—though it seems new and novel in 1987—is a staple of modern spread offenses.

Bengals starter Dave Walter was originally an eleventh-round pick[4] of the New York Giants and enters the game with modest passing stats, going eight for nineteen for ninety-eight yards in replacement action. His real value, though, came as a runner. The Bengals' lack of a passing game becomes apparent early, as Cleveland shuts down their running game with veterans like Sam Clancy flashing through to make tackles in the backfield.

Cincinnati fans seemed largely unaffected by the strike, as Riverfront Stadium is nearly full for this rivalry game, and through a quarter of game action there is little talk of the strike—either its impending end or its impact. Bengals defensive end Willie Fears is an example of the nomadic life of the replacement player. A standout college player at Northwestern State University, Fears was a prison guard at a maximum security facility before suiting up as a replacement player. He would play for the Bengals and Vikings in the NFL, the San Antonio Roughriders of the World League of American Football, and the Arena Football League's Cleveland Thunderbolts, Tampa Bay Storm, and Nashville Kats. Though he only played in five NFL games (in 1987 and 1990), Fears had a relatively long and relatively distinguished pro football career as a player and coach .[5]

"The Bengals probably had one of the highest solidarity levels of any of the NFL teams during the strike," says Breen. "The replacement players all stayed at the same hotel in downtown Cincinnati. Two buses picked us up every day and took us to and from practice. We had to rotate entrances at the old Spinney Practice Facility as the regular players greeted us by throwing rocks and eggs at us. My mom was worried sick as she received a daily dose of death threats from various callers."

Wyche's posture from the start seemed to be to remain as loyal as possible (in perception and even in the reality of play calling) to his regular players. Especially quarterback Boomer Esiason with whom he would have a rocky, but ultimately beneficial, relationship.

"Boomer Esiason and Dave Rimington were very vocal NFLPA reps and we sparred quite a bit in the local media and in public," Breen recalls. "The striking players used to wait for us in our hotel lobby [once they figured out where we were] and tried to intimidate us. Small altercations broke out until Sam Wyche called us in and threatened to cut us if we retaliated. Sam's allegiances were clearly with Boomer [rightfully so], and the entire situation aggravated him. We told Sam that *they* were the ones waiting for us; we were not the ones looking for a confrontation. His advice was just to walk away and ignore them."

Breen explains that the Bengals regulars even went so far as to take every pair of team shirts, shorts, and socks with a Bengals logo emblazoned on it—to the point that the team's equipment manager had to order plain gray shirts and shorts.

"The Bengals players that did cross the line [Williams and Edwards] were very supportive and told us the striking players would be doing exactly what we were doing if they were in our situation," Breen continues. "They said just to be a professional, block it out, and focus on the job at hand. We have a game to play on Sunday."

By early in the second quarter, Brennan has five catches for sixty-four yards and a score. He is having his way with Cincinnati's overmatched secondary, and his numbers are on pace with those being put up by Steve Largent a few hours to the north and west in the Pontiac Silverdome. The disparity between regular and replacement is perhaps best seen in those isolation battles between receivers and cornerbacks. Crafty veteran receivers like Brennan and Largent seem to be feasting on the relatively inexperienced replacements across the line of scrimmage.

Danielson is putting up career numbers as well, going 11 for 13 for 130 yards and a score through a quarter and a drive. He hits tight end Derek Tennell, a UCLA product, for a three-yard strike to run the score to 14–0. Tennell would stick on the regular roster after the strike, and would in fact go on to play in the league until 1993—his best year, when he caught fifteen passes as a Minnesota Viking.

A forced fumble by Alvin Horn gives Cleveland possession in Bengals territory yet again, where Danielson makes use of the bubble screen to Brennan on the first play of the series, picking up fourteen yards and a first down. The drive would end in a Jeff Jaeger field goal to send Cleveland up 17–0. Jaeger, a third-round pick of the Browns in 1987, would go on to kick in the league until 1999.

Before halftime, Ozzie Newsome extends his consecutive-games-with-a-catch streak to 117 games with catches on consecutive plays. Between Brennan, who set his career high with eight catches before halftime, and Ozzie Newsome running free in the secondary, it's hardly fair. Danielson, however, is struggling with the *simplicity* of the stripped-down Cleveland offense and has to write the play calls on his wristband during a break in the action. He even involves fullback Major Everett on a play-action rollout to pick up a first down, immediately before hitting Perry Kemp over the top on a deep scoring strike on a post pattern. Kemp made enough of an impression in his three replacement games to receive an opportunity with the Green Bay Packers in 1988, where he would log forty-eight receptions, along with another forty-eight in 1989.

The Bengals try shifting their backfield personnel near the end of the half in an attempt to get something going. They go with journeyman Ben Bennett, who would log significant AFL and WLAF (World League of American Football) time as well. Bennett's performance, however, is decidedly Dave Walter–like, and he goes three-and-out in his first series, giving Cleveland another opportunity to score before the half.

"Anyone who's knowledgeable about the game of professional football knows that anytime the players cross the white stripe, anything can happen," says Marty Schottenheimer on whether or not his veterans would give him an advantage. "Ask me after the ball game."

❈ ❈ ❈

One of Cincinnati's only bright spots on the field is 1986 NFL Man of the Year Reggie Williams, a linebacker from Dartmouth. One of only two regulars to cross the picket line for the Bengals (along with star defensive end Eddie Edwards), Williams angrily recovers a fumble to end the half and appears to be playing with an extra measure of fury.

Williams was a leader on and off the field for the Bengals. He would play 14 seasons, appear in 2 Super Bowls, and log 62.5 sacks, which is second all-time in club history. He would also serve two terms on the Cincinnati City Council in 1988 and 1989. Williams has endured twenty-four knee operations since the end of his playing career, many of those coming after 2008 as he struggled with multiple infections.

There was a spate of articles written about Williams a few years ago, as the media caught wind of his battle to keep his right leg, which is 2 5/8 inches shorter than the left after a portion of his femur was ravaged by osteomyelitis. He lives by himself in an apartment near Orlando, where each day involves an elaborate but necessary routine of stretching and heat and physical therapy that makes it possible for him to simply walk around a little—something he no longer takes for granted.

Wrote Paul Daugherty in a 2013 *USA Today* report, "His life is a continuous series of small, deliberate movements, a search for comfort and healing, an odyssey of maintenance and pain management. He does these things without complaint or assistance, because he understands that if he doesn't, his right leg will require amputation, and everything he has worked for his entire life will lose meaning."[6]

The report indicates that he eats no meals at home because doing so (shopping, cooking) requires so much standing, which would do further damage to his knee. He must also keep his Orlando apartment hot because air conditioning aggravates his knee.[7]

Life "having meaning" is a tricky thing to come by, much less quantify. By man's fallible standards, Williams has been extremely successful. Not many people can go to Dartmouth and then excel for almost a decade and a half in the world's most brutal sport, and then retire only to launch a successful Disney Sports complex.

Yet his body stands as a tribute to the entropy, loss, and pain that mark life in a fallen world. When we're young, we dream of pro football, and then we figure that those who star in the game go on to live a life of limousines and public appearances and radio shows and talking-head work on cable sports affiliates. We don't imagine them struggling to get up off their sofa and then just being thankful for another day where their leg isn't amputated. We don't, in a nutshell, expect to see them struggling with their own sense of meaning.

"It can take me five minutes to get to the door,"[8] he said.

Williams, in the *USA Today* report, also seemed uneasy about his place in Bengals history. Only one Bengals played in more games (206) than Williams, yet there are no megasized banners or statues of him outside Paul Brown Stadium. Even in his own era, he was overshadowed by the inception of the freakish pass rusher (Lawrence Taylor, Derrick Thomas), he was overshadowed by better linebacking units (the 1980s Bears and Giants), and was finally just overshadowed by *louder* players like Brian Bosworth. All Williams did, essentially, was play his position really well for a really long time for a franchise that was notoriously cheap and flew decidedly under the radar for most of the 1980s and 1990s, even while boasting the game's best left tackle in Anthony Munoz, and even while appearing in two Super Bowls. The

Bengals managed to stay irrelevant even when they were, technically, relevant.

So in spite of his relatively dominant playing career and his note-worthy success off the field, Williams exists in a sort of postathletic purgatory where the joy of the career is long past, but the fallout of it is a daily battle. It's a reminder of the Faustian pact made by the pro football player in which that player sometimes trades a stable, pain-free future for the thrill and money of the present.

In retirement, how much appreciation is enough? How many radio appearances, card shows, or endorsements are enough? It's a rhetorical question, but one that may be fundamentally unanswerable by those of us who don't limp in Williams's orthopedic shoes. Today, instead of adulation for his career, he is subject to curious glances at the lump of disfigured flesh between his femur and his tibia.

"I can learn a lot about a person by how they respond to my knee."[9]

❋ ❋ ❋

This is the first divisional game for both teams, both of whom came into the game 2–2, which brings into sharper focus the mismatch in talent, as Cleveland returned many of its regulars.

Adrian Breen's last day as a professional football player began, in a strange way, with the opening play of the second half. He wasn't a part of the play on the field, but he was blamed by the NBC crew for a long interception that was actually thrown by quarterback Ben Bennett.[10] It was the kind of long interception in which the quarterback simply throws the ball up for grabs and, in this case, there happened to be three Cleveland Browns and only one potential Bengals receiver in the area. Troy Wilson, a replacement player from Notre Dame, makes the interception. The network talking heads don't bother to correct their error, even as Ben Bennett is shown conversing with Wyche on the sidelines after the errant pass.

After the Browns take possession, replacement running back Larry Mason[11] runs a beautiful version of the "counter gap" play made famous a few years later by the Washington Redskins. On the counter gap, the backside guard and tackle pull to lead the ball carrier through an area vacated by the down-blocking front-side guard and tackle. Nearly every team had a version of this play in this era, and seeing it run here, to perfection, brings an unexpected nostalgic surge.

A few plays later, however, Mason is stripped of the football by linebacker David Ward,[12] and the Bengals have an opportunity to make a game of it once more. After two short Marc Logan inside runs, Bennett makes perhaps the most interesting Bengal play of the afternoon out of the shotgun on third down. Alex Carter, the Browns defensive end, leapfrogs over the top of Logan, who whiffs on his block, causing Bennett to scramble for his life. Consequently, he sort of just shotputs the ball over the head of a Browns defender to Logan, who finds himself running free for a first down. Logan would limp off the field, and it would be one of their last positive plays.

A Bengals fumble a few plays later is recovered by Browns nose tackle Mike Rusinek, who shares that coach Marty Schottenheimer struggled to learn his name, calling him "Paul" for a time, and then "Billy," and then finally "Billy-Paul," even though his given name is "Mike."

The Bengals front four is generating no rush, and on the rare occasion that they blitz, Danielson adjusts deftly and takes advantage, as he comes inches away from doing in the third quarter on a near-perfect fade that is an inch beyond Brennan's fingertips. On the ensuing fourth down, Schottenheimer goes for it, and Brennan collects his tenth reception and causes the same kind of record-related worry that is happening in Detroit via Steve Largent in that it would be a shame for significant team or league records to fall in a replacement game. The replacement Bengals are making Gary Danielson[13] look like Joe Montana.

"It was like watching Notre Dame take on Hillsdale Junior College," said Ernie Accorsi in *The GM*. "We were leading 34–0, it was pitch and catch, and Danielson had completed like twenty passes in a row, when suddenly it dawned on me that these records were going to count . . . I rushed into the coach's booth. I'd never done anything like that in my life. 'Tell Schottenheimer,' I shouted, 'to get Brennan the hell out of the game! We have sacred trust!'"[14]

Accorsi's vigilance would preserve the integrity of the Browns' team records, much to the chagrin of his receiver. "He was pissing and moaning on the sidelines, waving his fist at the press box."[15]

Browns regulars Sam Clancy and Carl Hairston, both defensive linemen, are absolutely owning the line of scrimmage, proving the importance of line play. Their penetration renders the Bengals run game nonexistent, and when Bennett tries to pass, he is forced to run for his life. One gets the sense, watching a game like this, that if these two particular teams played 100 times, the Browns would probably win 100 times, such is the talent disparity on the field. Through three quarters, the Bengals have eighty-six total yards, and the Browns have yet to punt the football.

In the fourth quarter, Danielson throws a perfect fade over Perry Kemp's left shoulder to run the score to 34–0.[16] Having been on the short end of games like this, I can tell you that the focus shifts from trying to score points to just trying to keep the clock running and get out of the game in one piece. Coaches and players would never say this, but it's true. Thus the Bengals' decision to line up in an I-formation and run the football when down 34–0 in the fourth quarter, sending Scott Fulhage on to punt for what seems like the eighty-fifth time.

The Bengals would go on to lose eleven games in 1987, many of them in the fourth quarter. Wyche's play calling was questioned. Though it is hard to believe watching this iteration of the club, the Bengals would be in the Super Bowl following the 1988 season, carried largely on the running of a thick rookie running back named Ickey Woods, who led the nation in rushing as a college senior at UNLV. He would become a minor and short-lived sensation, inventing a touchdown dance called "The Ickey Shuffle" in Week 6 against the Jets. "It kind of, like, took off like wildfire,"[17] said Woods. Even the venerable Paul Brown was moved by it, saying, "Personally I don't think much of it, but my wife likes it."[18] Woods led the AFC in yards-per-carry and touchdowns with fifteen. His running, at his size, evoked memories of other Bengals big-backs like Pete Johnson and Boobie Clark. This was perhaps the last Bengals team with an identity, as they christened Riverfront Stadium "The Jungle," and employed the catchphrase "Who dey?" along with the Ickey Shuffle. The Bengals were basically an invisible nonfactor during most of the 1990s and early 2000s, save for individual performances from players like Corey Dillon and Chad Johnson (née Ochocinco).

The 1988 Bengals Super Bowl team would take San Francisco to the wire in Super Bowl XXIII, which further cemented the big-game legacy of Joe Montana, who allegedly pointed out John Candy in the stands just before driving[19] his team down the field to a winning touchdown pass to John Taylor.

Meanwhile, Adrian Breen throws warm-up passes on the sideline, and his face, rather than showing excitement, is that of a man who may be heading to the firing squad. The Bengals have a total of three first downs in the game. On his first play, Breen runs a college-style triple-option, which the Browns diagnose and shut down perfectly. His stats on the season are a modest three for five for nine yards and a touchdown. This will be his last action as a professional football player.

"I signed with the then St. Louis Cardinals [now Arizona Cardinals] as a free agent right after the 1987 NFL Draft," says Breen, who is now the president/CEO at American National Bank. "I was cut/released by Gene Stallings after the first or second preseason game. When I turned my equipment in, they inventoried it and put it in a bag with my name on it. I remember asking why they did that, and the equipment manager told me he thought they might bring me back."

While the Cardinals were already making preparations to fill their replacement rosters, the Bengals were in the process of beating them to the punch.

"I headed back to Morehead State to complete my finance degree as I never redshirted and had thirteen hours remaining," Breen recalls. "Classes had already started so Coach Baldridge invited me to be a graduate assistant coach until the spring semester. One afternoon, my phone rang, and it was Frank Smouse [scout/assistant personnel director]. Frank told me he had been following me in St. Louis and to stay in shape; the Bengals were going to invite me to camp the following year. At the end of the conversation, Frank said, 'Let me ask you a hypothetical question. If there was a player's strike; would you consider crossing the picket line and playing for the Bengals?' I said yes, and the Bengals offered to honor my contract from St. Louis [$70,000–$75,000] and would be sending me a contract to sign. Once signed/received, they would send me a check for $10,000. If there was a strike, I played for the Bengals. If there was no strike, I was invited to camp the following year. This was three or four weeks prior to the actual players' strike. Paul Brown had a contingency plan and had assembled an entire team on paper weeks before the strike. Once the strike was actually announced, the St. Louis Cardinals called and invited me to return to the

Cardinals. I told them I had already signed with the Bengals and was looking forward to playing in my hometown."

Breen's history with the Bengals far predated his signing, as former Bengals quarterback Ken Anderson was instrumental in young Breen's development.

"One of my best friends from high school was Tom Gray," he says. "Tom's father was the longtime equipment manager for the Bengals. The Grays were like family to me, so it made the experience even more memorable. I never 'officially' went to camp with the Bengals, but Tom and I would go to Wilmington College [in between our own high school football schedule] where the Bengals held their summer camp. We volunteered to help out just to be there and take in the whole experience. I did not play QB until my sophomore year in high school [after Tom Gray injured his shoulder] so I needed a lot of work. In the evenings Ken Anderson used to come out and watch Tom and I throw/run routes and coached me on the mechanics of throwing a football, footwork and mental toughness."

His career lasts a series longer, as he is the beneficiary of a pass interference penalty, giving the Bengals the ball fairly deep in Cleveland territory. Like Bennett, Breen is forced to run for his life whenever he drops back to throw. He scrambles for nine yards and draws an unnecessary roughness penalty, bringing a first down inside the ten.

Breen, who played his high school football in Cincinnati, understands the magnitude of the rivalry. An opportunity for a touchdown pass flutters through the hands of Marc Logan on a catchable ball. He puts another pass right into the hands of his receiver on a slant and doesn't get an interference call. Finally, he throws a fade for Greg Meehan that looks like a score, only to find out that Meehan trapped the football on the threadbare turf. The football gods[20] seem intent on keeping Breen out of the end zone. On fourth and goal, Breen is sacked by Mike Rusinek, and with that, his career is over. Still, he has no regrets.

"Sports in general played a big part in my life and development as a person and business leader," he says. "Character, teamwork, hard work, and mental toughness are the obvious lessons. The importance of strategy, planning, coaching, adaptability, and having a good system are also key. My management philosophy today was crafted from my sports experience."

Breen has even drawn from the tedium of daily football practice to enrich his company's environment.

"The foundation for a team's daily practice routine—doing individual work first, then position groups, then finally team—is a great outline to follow for building a successful organization," he says. "Individual talent, aspirations, and skills aligned with group goals and expectations, ultimately cascade into the team's performance."

Breen and the replacement Bengals trudged to the locker room after the game, feeling as though they'd let their owner down. He would never play football again, as he found out a year later that he had actually fractured a vertebra.

"Brown said, 'You fought until the last whistle blew,'" Breen recalls. "He said, 'Take your uniforms. Thanks for all that you did.'"

AFTERWORD

The Running Man: Walter Payton, Brian Bosworth, and Childhood Heroes

My wife and I often say things like, "I can't believe we're adults . . . I don't feel old enough to_____ [have kids, have a house, etc.]." Which raises the question: What does it mean to be grown up?

In part, the answer came to me as I was reading *Sweetness* by Jeff Pearlman. It's a book I'd previously and very intentionally avoided like the plague. You see, Walter Payton—"Sweetness"—was my childhood hero. The 1970s vintage *Sports Illustrated* poster of Payton (gray face mask, elbow pads, AstroTurf) hung in my room for years until it was joined by another poster of Payton running up a steep hill he famously ran up in order to prepare for the upcoming season. Payton was famous for his work ethic and supposed selflessness, and I wanted to emulate those things myself. Payton was the guy who played hurt, who didn't care about stats, and who would keep battling when everyone else fell out. And he did it with a smile on his face. Sweetness.

I had read that Pearlman's book would deconstruct many of those fond memories, and much of the intentionally crafted Payton public image (family man, Christian, etc.), hence the avoidance. However, my curiosity and almost unquenchable desire for football books got the best of me.

If you were a sports fan in the 1980s and/or are from the Chicago area, this book will be a treasure trove of fascination for you. Pearlman did his homework, interviewing scads of former Bears including Brian Baschnagel, Cliff Thrift, and Roland Harper (again, names that will only matter to you if you were a Bears fan, but if you were a Bears fan, they'll mean a great deal to you). Honestly, hearing from these guys may have been the most charming thing about this book. I spent more time thinking about Bob Avellini, Vince Evans, and Mike Phipps as a result of this book than anyone should. The dreadfulness of late 1970s Bear quarterbacking is almost a book unto itself.

Regarding adulthood—reading and processing a book like this, that deconstructs one's childhood heroes, is what it means to be grown up. I'm not a nine-year-old crying in my room because Walter Payton disappointed me. Still, there is a feeling of sadness after reading this book in which I learned that Payton took too many painkillers, chased too many women on the road, and wasn't really close with any of his teammates despite his smiley and chummy exterior. I learned that he cared a little bit too much about his own statistics. I learned that many of the 1980s-vintage Bears were steroid users. I learned that there was a great deal of dissension and selfishness in the locker room. I learned that much of Payton's public image was very carefully and successfully crafted by his agent. I learned that Payton—the NFL's all-time leading rusher, a Super Bowl champion, and the undisputed king of Chicago sports—struggled mightily with depression postcareer.

Did any of this come as a huge surprise? Not really. There's plenty of public sadness and tragedy in sports, and the 1985 Bears are no different. There have been bankruptcies, DUIs, and just public embarrassments of every stripe and color.

It occurs to me that this is what it means to be an adult: The realization that nothing, and no one, is perfect in the great escapist activity that is sports. As great as Walter Payton was (courageous, charismatic, etc.), he was even more sinful and flawed. He needed redemption and peace as much as someone like Mike Tyson, who wears his flaws on his sleeve. He was living proof that widespread popularity, insane professional achievement, and universal "love" wasn't enough to fulfill him or assuage the sadness. It wasn't enough to bring any real community to the Bears' locker room.

The book, initially, bummed me out. But as a result of the book I've YouTubed (verb) old Bears games and old Payton highlight packages. I've been reminded of how sensational and courageous Payton was. I've

marveled at the collection of talent on Buddy Ryan's defenses. I've
repurchased my old poster on eBay. And once again, the gifts that God
bestowed on Walter Payton have brought me joy.

❖ ❖ ❖

"I can't believe I still have this," said a tearful Brian Bosworth in an
ESPN 30 for 30 documentary called *Brian and the Boz*. "This is something I'm not proud of. This is not who I am. And I've apologized to my
teammates and my school and my coach because of this."

He is the picture of brokenness and contrition. "If there is one thing
I could take back . . . I would take this back. Sometimes it's good to
have reminders of the mistakes you make . . . so I'll keep it."

He is speaking of a t-shirt emblazoned with "National Communists
Against Athletes," which he infamously wore to the 1987 Rose Bowl
game—a game from which he was suspended because of a positive
steroid test. The basis of the documentary frames Bosworth in a rented
storage locker belonging to his father, Foster. It contains the totality of
Bosworth's public life—a collection of news clippings, t-shirts, jerseys,
footballs, and helmets. It contains the totality of a father's worship. In
the film, Bosworth is the docent, while his son takes it all in like an
interested tourist. The effect is fascinating.

Bosworth summed up the era best as he was showing a photograph
to his son of himself, in sunglasses, on a media day podium surrounded
by reporters shoving microphones in his face. "Awesome," said his son.
"You see 'awesome,' but I see lost," the Boz replies. "I'm up here trying
to be a deity. But I'm just a football player."

For me, the 1987 season ended with Payton's playoff loss in Chicago,
but there is still much of The Boz and Sweetness in me. These two men
were the 1980s to me. They represented everything I thought I wanted
to be, back when I thought like a child and reasoned like a child.
Bosworth's tears flow freely in this documentary as he shares his sins
with his son. It occurs to me that I've never been prouder of a childhood hero.

In a classic shot that freezing afternoon in 1987, Walter Payton sat
alone on the Chicago bench with his helmeted head in his hands.
Everything about Payton looked old—his small shoulder pads, his

1970s-vintage Wilson helmet, and even his elbow pads. He sat on the bench and wept, alone.

In our den in Hartford City, Indiana, I sat on my sofa and wept, too.

EPILOGUE

Over the Top: 1987 and Beyond

Walter Payton's last regular season game[1] took place in Chicago against rookie Brian Bosworth and the Seattle Seahawks. It was a confluence of styles—Payton's grit and understatedness set against Bosworth's flash and market-mindedness. It was not only a confluence of styles but a passing of the torch as Payton's era ended and Bosworth ushered in a newer, more market-savvy era in which athletes like Bo Jackson and Michael Jordan would be packaged as shoe-and-clothing salesmen and would leave a permanent mark on pop culture as a result. The 1990s would bring Payton-esque throwbacks like Barry Sanders and (to some degree) Emmitt Smith, but this was the end of an era.

I find the Bears vs. Seahawks game in a box of old VHS tapes, the box still covered with my eleven-year-old scrawl. I pop the tape in and discover that I've captured some of the pregame show, which features Brent Musburger, who has changed very little in the last twenty-five years in that he is still selling the idea that each game is a life-and-death experience. He is joined by Jimmy "The Greek" Snyder, who had a segment called "The Greek's Corner" in which he handicaps games for gamblers and is sort of the bumbling "wise guy" figure who occasionally forgets the names of players but wears a great pair of semitinted glasses à la Mike Ditka in the 1980s. I'm reminded that the NFL no longer acknowledges the existence of gambling in its official broadcasts. The

Greek proves prophetic, though, as he correctly picks The Boz and Seattle to top a banged-up Bears squad.

The pregame show also features a young Dick Vermeil, who at the time had left coaching due to burnout, but who would go on to win a Super Bowl with the St. Louis Rams and quarterback Kurt Warner. Compared to modern pregame shows, which seem to be a guffawing-ex-player arms race, there is precious little guffawing and even less attempted cleverness. It's refreshing. Even the set is taupe and understated.

Journalist Will McDonough profiles his top prospects for the 1988 draft, is "right" on an astonishing number of prospects, including Keith Jackson, Bennie Blades, and Tim Brown. He is really only "wrong" on bust pass-rusher Aundray Bruce out of Auburn. McDonough's piece ends with the statement, "There's no way we'll have instant replay after this year." We, of course, still have it twenty-five years later, and it is still annoying.[2]

On field, Walter Payton's jersey is retired by the Chicago Bears before the game, putting him in company with players like Red Grange (77), Bronco Nagurski (3), and Bulldog Turner (66). "I never thought it would end like this," says Payton during the ceremony. "When I started playing this game, I did it because I loved it and it was fun. That's the same reason I'm playing now, because I love it and it's fun. I guess the hardest thing to do is to say goodbye to those you love. Those guys standing down there in the end zone are my love. Thanks for being there."

The on-field temperature is a fitting thirty-four degrees. Injured quarterback Jim McMahon stalks the sidelines in a flamboyant fur coat, accented with leather and fringe. Payton opens the game in the same backfield as Neal Anderson, who would be his heir apparent. Payton, clearly aging, averaged only 3.4 yards per carry on the season—a full yard beneath his career average. "I think the strike really hurt him," says analyst Merlin Olsen. "That four-week layoff hurt him."

Payton is a buzz saw on the opening drive and collides with Bosworth often. Chicago knows that it is not going to bring Seattle's defense to its knees with a passing game featuring Mike Tomczak, Willie Gault, and Ron Morris. It is Payton or bust. At the end of Chicago's first series, a former New Orleans Saints replacement player, Tommy Barnhart, punts the ball away.

"There's the difference between the Payton of a few years ago and the Payton of today," says Dick Enberg after Payton is chopped down by Bosworth on an off-tackle run in the first quarter. The Bears appear out of sync and disoriented as Tomczak is the architect of a handful of broken plays.

Between segments, there are advertisements for the upcoming Rose Bowl game featuring a young Michigan State offensive tackle named Tony Mandarich, who would build on both the marketing and banned-substance legacy started by Bosworth. If Bosworth was football's first cool white guy since Joe Namath, Mandarich was its first cool offensive lineman. For a moment, he would bend popular culture in a similar way. As an audience member with a unique perspective on lame, Mid-western white guys (being that I was one), we adored Boz and Manda-rich because they had the audacity to rise above the anonymity of their positions and dare, for a while, to be known. Of course, it is an act that can quickly grow thin. Namath was one of the few who had the staying power to pull it off for a long time, and even so, there were anti-Namath factions in his own locker room.

There is a very thinly veiled, anti-Bosworth sentiment that runs through the game's telecast, particularly when analyst Merlin Olsen is talking about other players on the Seahawks defense. "Make no mistake, Fredd Young is the star of this defense," Olsen[3] says after Bosworth's linebacking counterpart makes a play. There is praise abounding for Jacob Green, Young, and fellow rookie Tony Woods, but little love for Bosworth. "I bet he's glad they're not paying him by the play," says Olsen, later, barely disguising his Boz-related disgust.

"It hasn't been fun in Seattle," said Bosworth of his rookie year in the spotlight—proof that fame and millions can't buy happiness. His 1987 was marked and will be remembered by a Monday Night Football nightmare in which he was run over on the goal line by Raiders sensation Bo Jackson, who famously referred to football as his hobby (Jackson also played professional baseball for the Kansas City Royals).

Seattle's offense is every bit as big and physical as Chicago's once-fearsome defense. They bludgeon the Chicago front with Kurt Warner and fullback John L. Williams, and they do so behind a very large and physical offensive line. Their quarterback is far-better-than-average Dave Krieg, who has the luxury of throwing to a future Hall of Famer in Steve Largent. The Seahawks draw first blood on a Krieg to Darryl

Turner back-shoulder fade (before that was a "thing") for a touchdown. The Chicago offense, by contrast, hadn't had a score of any kind in six quarters of football.

Turnovers would prove to be the story of the game, as Chicago would lose five (three fumbles, two Tomczak picks) to Seattle's zero. Bosworth makes his presence felt, tomahawking Tomczak to the turf in the second quarter and nearly returning a fumble for a touchdown to open the third on a play in which he simultaneously tackled and separated Bear running back Neal Anderson from the football. He is generally regarded as a "bust" because of his injury-shortened career, but this game is proof that Bosworth really could play. He is a playmaking presence throughout,[4] and truth be told, was for most of his rookie year. However, with the ascension of rushers like Lawrence Taylor, the NFL was moving away from the middle-linebacker-centric defenses of the previous decade and beginning to feature players who could rush off the edge.

This game was a quiet end to the career of linebacker Keith Butler, who was first to congratulate Bosworth after his fumble return as NBC flashed a Bosworth quote onto the screen that read, "The football field is my stage. It's where I perform."

The poor weather that Ditka had hoped for never came, and the sunshine and relative calm allowed Krieg to throw the short timing routes on which his offense thrived. Payton rushed for a respectable seventy-nine yards on seventeen carries, but far from his dominant performances of the past. It is his eighteenth-straight game without 100 yards rushing. However, his beautiful, nifty touchdown run in the third quarter is vintage, and he fires the ball into the crowd after the score. It wouldn't be enough.

After the score, Payton walked to the end of the bench to kiss his injured heir apparent, Neal Anderson, on the top of the forehead.

The feel-good quickly dissipates as soon as Seattle takes possession, in the form of a seventy-five-yard touchdown catch-and-run by Seahawk running back John L. Williams.

After the 34–21 loss to Seattle, there was the feeling, on one hand, that life remained in Chicago, as Payton would have one more opportunity in the divisional playoff versus Washington. There was also, however, the feeling that the era was already over. And that perhaps the 1987 Bears lacked magic.

Payton lost his last professional game—an NFC divisional playoff clash with the eventual Super Bowl champion Washington Redskins—to end Chicago's 1987 season.

The telecast is another nostalgic trip, starting with the pregame dialogue between Snyder and Musburger in which Snyder, in trying to sum up quarterback Jim McMahon's impact on the Bears, says he "brings chaos, brings excitement." Unfortunately, he only brought it about half the time, as by 1987, McMahon's best days were already long over, lost in an avalanche of injuries. Incidentally, Snyder predicted that the Bears would beat Washington by a score of 23–20.

The game was preceded by a local WLS documentary on Payton that was mostly worshipful, and sometimes insightful. The picture it paints is of Payton the humanitarian, the businessman,[5] and the conquering athletic hero. It chronicles his league MVP season in 1977, and his 1981 season in which he carried the ball over forty times per game several times, his body bearing an unfathomable amount of punishment. There are appreciative interview segments with Jim Brown, and ironically, a pre-scandal O. J. Simpson, who, at that time, was as clean cut and "wholesome" as any professional athlete.

The program explains that Payton was "the first black to appear on breakfast tables across the country" on Wheaties boxes.

Doug Williams leads the Redskins in the brutal Chicago cold, gloves on both hands. McMahon and company jog onto the field to a gladiatorial roar from the Chicago faithful. The old columns in Soldier Field just add to the Roman metaphor. Safety Dave Duerson is shown pummeling the goalpost pad to psyche himself up, pregame. He's now dead, of a suicide that was possibly brought about by repeated football-related head traumas.

I'm watching the game in my basement, which is home to the only remaining working VCR in my home. I found the old VHS tapes in a box someplace, and this tape is a treasure. My kids are sitting with me on an old basement sofa, riveted to the cheesy 1980s commercials[6] and the retro presentation. They're being introduced to the fact that before John Madden was a video game icon, he was once a football analyst because he was once a coach.

Kevin Butler, Chicago's moon-faced kicker,[7] boots the opening kickoff in a helmet without a chin strap. Chicago's defense was much like that of the dominant 1985 squad, with a few changes. Future Carolina Panthers head coach Ron Rivera had replaced Otis Wilson at outside linebacker, and "The Refrigerator," William Perry, is conspicuously absent. "Where's the Fridge?" asks my eleven-year-old. The Bears mystique, like the logo painted on the AstroTurf at Soldier Field, had already faded.

The Redskins win with a punishing running game, winning their last thirty-five straight when they've had a back rush for over 100 yards. The Bear defense, by contrast, hadn't allowed a 100-yard rusher in twenty-three games.

The Bears go deep on their first two offensive plays, both of which were McMahon misfires. McMahon scrambles on third and long and loses his helmet,[8] forcing a Tommy Barnhardt punt to future Hall of Famer Darrell Green. The boys love Madden bloviating about how "everything on you freezes" in cold weather, including "your spit, your sweat, and even your gloves!"

Payton's first carry is on a beautifully blocked sweep around the left end, behind a perfect lead block from fullback Matt Suhey, who was Payton's best friend off the field. The play goes for fifteen yards and features the trademark Payton leg kick, which would be reproduced, by me, many times in the backyard. Calvin Thomas's touchdown to cap the drive reminds me of how the Chicago Bears had a traveling basketball team that would roam the Midwest in the off-season in the 1980s, playing local police departments and the like. Thomas and the Bears basketballers came to my tiny Indiana town and played a game in the early 1980s, nearly causing a riot in our tiny town. It was big news.

John Madden, on stomach-related anxiety: "I had those tumbleations in there."

Mike Singletary starches Redskins running back George Rodgers[9] on a fourth and one and then removes his helmet to reveal a frozen[10] 1980s-style moustache. Payton starts the ensuing series with another sweep. He had been increasingly phased out of the offense, rushing for just over 500 yards and a 3.7 average—both numbers supremely un-Payton-like. Still, in this game, he runs with what seems like an extra spring in his step. He picks up another twenty yards on a draw play, prompting CBS to display a primitive graphic showing a cartoon Payton running up Mount Everest, back down, and then back up again. I distinctly remember the graphic from 1987 thinking, at age eleven, how very cool it was. It apparently lodged itself somewhere in my subconscious.

"There's a fired-up guy," says Madden of Payton. Midway through the second quarter, Payton's heir apparent, Neal Anderson, has yet to see the field, and the Bears are outrushing Washington sixty-five yards to eight.

Madden: "That's the kind of quarterback McMahon is! Throw it to one guy and another guy gets it! So what! Who cares! Big deal!"

The halftime score is 14–14, thanks largely to the passing of Doug Williams on the Washington side and the running of Walter Payton for Chicago. At halftime, Dick Butkus appears in a parka that makes him look like Nanook of the North, and a very somber Will McDonough reports on Bears injuries, standing outside the locker room door, which was a very "1980s" technique, as though proximity to the door suggested unique information.

The underrated Redskins defense, led by Charles Mann, Dexter Manley, and Daryl Grant, put constant pressure on McMahon in the second half and eventually closed the door on Sweetness and the Bear running game. McMahon's ugly interception to Brian Davis to open the second half was just a foretaste of things to come. The dominant 1985 Bear squad was an impressive +23 in turnovers, while the 1987 squad is -20. In many ways it's remarkable they made it this far.

The Bears are effectively done when Darrell Green returns a punt for a touchdown in the third quarter. He pulls a muscle in his rib cage on the return and runs the final twenty yards clutching his side but scores anyway. The mood at Soldier Field has shifted discernibly, as it seems as though Bears players and fans are collectively pondering the fact that Payton will retire and McMahon will soon be gone. The Bears, for the first time, look cold, defeated, and human. The swagger is gone, and even though I'm not eleven anymore, there are still pangs of sadness.

* * *

The Redskins were beneficiaries of momentum gained during the strike games, and some inspired performances by their replacement players, including quarterbacks Ed Rubbert and Tony Robinson.[11] Rubbert, winner of all of his starts, went 26–49 for 531 yards and 4 touchdowns with only one pick. Despite his strong showing, he would never again appear in an NFL game. Replacement wideout Anthony Allen set a single-game record with 7 catches for 255 yards and 3 touchdowns.

The Redskins were one of only three teams to win all of their strike games and sat atop the NFC East at 4–1 when the strike ended. They were prepared for the strike weeks largely due to the preparation of their general manager, Bobby Beathard, who said of the process of building a replacement team from scratch, "It's almost like another draft . . . it was a lot of fun."[12]

Redskins leadership, in step with many of the other owners, expressed that the league was more than the players, and that the game would indeed go on, with or without them. "The players association thought they had the upper hand in negotiations, and their mantra was that they are the game," said John Kent Cooke, the Redskins' executive vice president at the time and the son of then-owner Jack Kent Cooke. "We decided to have replacement squads just to show the regular players they were not the game, but an integral part of the game, and that the league would go on no matter who the players were."[13]

"They broke our backs," said regular linebacker Neil Olkewicz of circumstances like the networks continuing to televise games and fans continuing (at some level) to show up. "It wasn't a fun time. We caved in."[14]

Former Redskins safety (and former NFLPA union rep) Mark Murphy explained the situation succinctly, saying, "They had to come up with something to negate the effectiveness of the strike. We felt at the time the replacements would risk the credibility of the NFL, but they were effective in the sense that they allowed the owners to continue to have the games on TV. It put a lot of pressure on us, and players started crossing the picket line."

Poststrike, the Redskins weathered a quarterbacking change (Doug Williams replacing Jay Schroeder) and upheaval at the running back position that would have unheralded rookie backup tailback Timmy Smith setting a Super Bowl rushing record and Doug Williams making history as the first African American quarterback to win a Super Bowl in a rout over John Elway's Denver Broncos.

1987 may have been the apex for the idea of the overly dramatic ballad (see every late-1980s television commercial), and as such, the NFL Films highlight package for the 1987 season and Redskins Super

Bowl victory features a treacly ballad crooned by a Luther Vandross knockoff playing over the highlights that are usually accompanied by the orchestral soundtrack of Sam Spence and company. It is unspeakably lame, and to my knowledge, they never did it again. The chorus was something like, "It's a long, hard road . . . now you're on the road to the Super Bowl!"[15]

"Sunday, October 4 was the most peculiar day in NFL history," says the film's narrator. "The real players were on strike, and a group of total strangers was trying to take their place."

"The names are unfamiliar," says Pat Summerall on the film. "It's almost like doing a college game or the first preseason game."

"With their motley assortment of cops and car salesmen, brick layers and bartenders, teams had to start over from square one," the narrator intones.

Houston Oilers head coach Jerry Glanville explains that he had nineteen players present at his first practice, three of whom were quarterbacks, two of whom quit the next day. Glanville brought some much-needed humor and personality to the league and led the Oilers to a playoff berth after a long drought.

The film then featured a mash-up of all of the follies—fumbles, interceptions, and other gaffes—generated during the three weeks of strike football. It's fascinating to see the league's spin on this period. My eight-year-old son endearingly refers to these clips simply as "drop the football."

"It was almost like forming a new league, but you had to do it in ten days," says Beathard. "We thought maybe we'll be able to take advantage of something like this."

1987 saw the ascension of several traditionally moribund franchises, including the Colts and the New Orleans Saints, who enjoyed the first winning season in the history of the franchise. They also enjoyed a series of quotes by head coach Jim Mora including his famous "we're just not good enough" press conference in Week 7. The Saints were led by resurrected USFL quarterback Bobby Hebert and a savage linebacking corps including Vaughn Johnson, Pat Swilling, and another former USFL standout in Sam Mills.

The Redskins, 11–4, won the NFC East and clinched a playoff berth sooner than any other team, yet they did so without flash. In discussions of elite teams in 1987, they were often left out. In the AFC, John Elway passed the Denver Broncos into the Super Bowl, as the team lacked a running game and the defense featured seven players in new positions. They beat Glanville's Oilers to advance to the AFC Championship berth against the Cleveland Browns.

Browns head coach Marty Schottenheimer had led the Browns to three straight AFC Central titles, championing a football theory that wasn't nearly as glamorous and star-centric as the one Elway found himself in. It would later be called "Martyball," and was built around no-nonsense, smashmouth, hard running. Martyball wasn't sexy. It featured two big, strong running backs and seemed perfectly suited to the swirling winds and muddy turf in Cleveland. Ironically, the 1987 AFC Championship would be decided in part by one of Martyball's biggest beneficiaries.

The Browns were led onto the field by native son Bernie Kosar, whose thin, gawky athletic stature belied a deep inner resolve and an odd sort of effectiveness. He was as rusty as Elway was golden. Kosar was a hero in Cleveland in no small part because he actually *wanted* to live and play there in a time when the city seemed to be on its economic (and athletic) last leg. Cleveland traded its first-round picks in 1985 and 1986 for the right to select him in the 1985 supplemental draft.

Kosar was sacked[16] on the game's first play. It was a harbinger of things to come. After the sack, they began chopping away at Denver's defense with running backs Kevin Mack and Earnest Byner, who was described as "the heart" of the Cleveland offense,[17] and also referred to by Schottenheimer as "the last man I would trade." The outcome of this game would, perhaps, forever change that sentiment. It would certainly change Byner's life.

Broncos head coach Dan Reeves was participating in his eleventh championship game as a player and coach. By the time the championship games kicked off, the strike seemed a long-ago unpleasant memory. Elway struck first, hitting wideout Ricky Nattiel in the end zone in the first quarter after a Cleveland turnover. It was fitting that the game began with a score off a fumble and would end in much the same fashion. Incidentally, Denver's old uniform—orange jersey, white pants, light-blue helmet with the "D" logo—is sublime. Sometime in the late 1990s, they replaced it with something that looks like it belongs in the Arena Football League and have, inexplicably, stayed loyal to the new design ever since.

Though Denver led for the duration of the game, Kosar and Byner kept the Browns in it. In the fourth quarter, Kosar led the team on an eighty-seven-yard drive, which culminated in a touchdown pass to Webster Slaughter. Fundamentally, everything was wrong about the scoring slant he threw to Slaughter—he was off balance and threw off his back foot. Still, in Kosar fashion, it was effective. He was a perfectly efficient ten-for-ten to start the second half. The score was preceded by a sublime fourteen-yard Kevin Mack run in which he willed his way inside the Denver ten-yard line, breaking several tackles along the way. He and Byner embodied the Martyball ethic.

Elway quickly countered, however, with his own twenty-yard scoring strike to Sammy Winder and was sensational in directing his scoring drive. The drive featured classic late-1980s matchups including Denver wide receiver Ricky Nattiel[18] working on Cleveland's elite corner, Hanford Dixon. But Winder's touchdown catch was less a function of Elway brilliance and more just a great piece of open-field running by the underrated back. He is often (wrongly) associated with an era in which Denver couldn't run the ball, but scored this (eventual winning) touchdown on his own. He outraced former Cleveland replacement linebacker, David Grayson, to the end zone pylon.

With four minutes left, the Browns took over again, with one final opportunity to produce a score-tying touchdown. Byner began the drive with a 19-yard run and he would end an otherwise sensational game with 7 receptions for 120 yards and 2 scores, to go with 67 yards rushing. He was referred to as "The Money Man" by analyst Merlin Olsen during the final drive, but it was what happened at the end of the drive that would forever define the running back.

The clock continued its slow slide toward zero as Cleveland moved over the frozen, confetti-littered gray turf. Strike-game hero Brian Brennan caught consecutive passes for key first downs right before the two-minute warning. There's a minimalistic symmetry and flow to the conclusion of this game, in that it's not continually interrupted by replay, coaches' challenges, and overanalysis. The network (NBC) seemed content to simply let the story of the game tell itself. The story took a drastic turn with 1:12 remaining. Earnest Byner took a handoff at the eight-yard line on a draw play and seemed on his way to another brilliant, tackle-breaking run. However, Byner lost the ball at the two-yard line, stripped of it by Denver's Jeremiah Castille as he (Byner) held it away from his body for the briefest of moments. He lay motionless on the gray turf for a few moments, seemingly unsure as to what to do with this turn of events. Often, the exhausted athlete seems less affected by these moments, as it is usually the media that gets ahold of something like this and blows it out of proportion. But Byner, despite his exhaustion and his heroic play throughout, seemed to sense it immediately. The man his coach said would never be traded was dealt to the Washington Redskins before the 1989 season, in exchange for little-used running back Mike Oliphant. Byner would make a Pro Bowl appearance and win a Super Bowl as a Redskin, and would return to the Browns in 1994.

✿ ✿ ✿

Super Bowl XXII was played in San Diego's Jack Murphy Stadium, which has always been, in my opinion, one of the more awesome NFL stadiums in that it has multiple "decks" and just always looked super huge and expansive. It also survived the lame "everybody rip down their not-even-old-yet stadiums and build a new one" trend that started in the 2000s. I love these overwrought NFL Films Super Bowl highlights tapes, all of which (in that era) were given titles like actual films. This one is called "Ambush at Super Bowl XXII" and featured the requisite F-14 flyover before the national anthem, the subtext of which is "there is nothing more American than what you're about to see."

It was an interesting confluence of styles. The Redskins were perceived as the ultimate team—lots of great parts, but essentially starless, while the Broncos were viewed simply as John Elway and forty-four other guys. Elway was one of the league's rising stars in 1987, having gamed the NFL Draft in 1983, refusing to play for the moribund Colts and brokering his trade to Denver. It would have been perceived as the ultimate jerk move had it not worked out perfectly.

"He was the best prospect I had ever seen," said then-Colts GM Ernie Accorsi. "If I was going to trade him, it was going to be for the greatest trade in the history of pro football." Within days of the draft the asking price for Elway was beginning to soften. The deal included solid offensive tackle Chris Hinton, journeyman quarterback Mark Herrman, and the number-one pick in 1984. Accorsi found out about the trade while watching the NBA playoffs on television. The deal happened without his approval.

In many ways, Elway's deal was quintessentially "1980s" in that it was self-serving and happened outside the confines of NFL convention, which dictated that you were to act overjoyed and "happy to be there" when you were drafted by whomever. Like Gordon Gekko, Elway realized he had leverage and used that leverage to his advantage. In a way, it was a precursor to what his coworkers would try to accomplish four years later during the 1987 strike—the freedom to choose where to live and work. Or, at least, a little more freedom than they'd previously enjoyed.

"I had to do what was best for John Elway," he said at the time, referring to himself in the third person. The trade may have been the death blow to the Baltimore Colts, as they moved out of town under the cover of night the following year.

The Broncos lined up in a shotgun formation on the first play of the game, and Elway fired a touchdown pass on a fifty-six-yard bomb to Ricky Nattiel. Washington, by contrast, looked tight and did nothing on its first quarter offensive possessions. Elway even caught a pass on Denver's next offensive series. The Broncos went up 10–0 on a Rich Karlis field goal.

But rather than go into the tank, the Redskins defense realized that taking away the pass essentially meant taking away the entire Denver offense. Their second-quarter offensive output was, of course, legendary. Doug Williams tossed scores to Ricky Sanders[19] and Gary Clark, and Washington's "hogs" began to maul the undersized Denver defense, clearing paths for the unheralded Timmy Smith. Smith had never started an NFL game prior to Super Bowl XXII, and even had the "look" of a rookie backup—his helmet didn't appear to fit quite right, his jersey was big and baggy, and even his number, 36, looked out of place and insignificant. But by the end of the second quarter, the score was 35–10, and the game was, for all practical purposes, over. The Redskins had amassed 243 yards and 5 touchdowns in a quarter of football.

Williams, who had spent most of the season on the bench, was frighteningly accurate, and the Redskins ran the counter gap what seemed like about a million times in a row. Timmy Smith[20] finished with 204 yards on 22 carries, breaking Marcus Allen's Super Bowl rushing record. Watching their huge offensive linemen pulling and trapping was a thing of beauty. Elway was sacked five times as Washington blitzed on every play. It was one of the worst Super Bowls in history from a "being close" standpoint, but the other story lines (Williams, Smith, etc.) redeemed it.

* * *

It's January 11, 2015, and I'm enjoying the Divisional Round of this season's NFL playoffs like many in my generation—while on the go and while doing something else. Since 1987, the NFL has become omnipresent, being that it is impossible to go anywhere in the greater Green Bay area (I'm here speaking at a conference) without encountering the following:

- A flat-screen television on a wall, showing either a game, pregame hype, or postgame postmortem.
- A grown man in an NFL jersey. Most attendees at my Sunday morning talk were wearing Packers jerseys, the subtext of which was, "Let's keep this talk short."
- A man, woman, or child streaming NFL-related content onto a mobile device.

The NFL has succeeded in being everywhere, all the time, while the players, as it turned out, succeeded in achieving higher salaries and the free agency they so coveted in 1987. For example, St. Louis Rams quarterback Sam Bradford, widely regarded as one of the least-effective and least-desirable starters in the league, has a contract valued at a shade over $78,000,000. Middling defensive end Calais Campbell (Arizona) has a contract worth $55,000,000. Journeyman right tackle Gosder Cherilus of the Indianapolis Colts has the twenty-fifth-richest contract in the league, which will pay him $35,000,000. He has never made a Pro Bowl but does, apparently, have an amazing agent. Disappointing Colts running back Trent Richardson rushed for only 519 yards for a 3.3 yards-per-carry average, but his 2015 contract is guaranteed, regardless of his roster spot. He is a healthy scratch today.

Richardson's backup, Dan Herron, quietly outplayed him in 2014, averaging 4.5 yards per carry in an increasing role down the stretch. He cost the Colts a relatively thrifty $570,000 in 2014. Herron is set to become a free agent, meaning that his initial contract will expire and he will be free to test his value on the open market, though it would behoove the Colts to bring him back. The Colts' "qualifying offer" will be at a salary level predetermined by the current collective bargaining agreement, and then Herron can solicit offers from other clubs. What he's about to experience is what players were fighting for in 1987. He will suddenly control just a little bit more of his own destiny and can make a decision based on geography, playing time, coaching staff, or (most likely) money.

The fallout of all of this is, of course, player movement, which makes it harder for the Detroit Lions fan who dropped $100 on his Ndamukong Suh jersey three years ago to see the Lions let him walk in free agency. As a result, fans make fewer personal connections with players, and are, rather, cheering for laundry (jerseys) on Sunday afternoons while their real personal connections with players come via fantasy teams. But via the fantasy product, the NFL has found a way to not only mitigate against but monetize the potentially damaging fan-effects of player movement. Simply stated, they make you care, one way or another.

As I make my way through the Detroit Metro Airport, I glance toward television monitors every few paces to see NFL quarterbacking royalty, Peyton Manning, taking a beating against his old team (Indianapolis). Our free-agent-to-be, Herron, rushes for sixty-three yards and a touchdown, while the aging Manning struggles to throw strikes in the cold Denver air. For the first time, he looks old, vulnerable, and perhaps even disinterested. Manning put professional football in Indianapolis on the map (as it were) in 1998, when he joined the Colts as the number-one overall pick in the draft. Now he and Herron are two ships passing in the night, probably not more than vaguely aware of each other, and headed in completely different directions.

The televisions are also ablaze (as is social media) with reports of another controversial instant replay call—the second in as many weeks—which will no doubt provide days' worth of fodder for online and on-air arguments, which (arguments) seem to be the very air we breathe these days as fans. With Manning's impending retirement, the league will have one less link to another era—an era without social media, fantasy football, or around-the-clock full-time coverage. It seems strange and somewhat inappropriate to be saying my football goodbyes to a legend from the Delta terminal at Detroit Metro.

I already miss Manning, as I miss the uncluttered simplicity of 1987.

NOTES

INTRODUCTION

1. CBS Sports telecast, October 4, 1987.
2. NBC Sports telecast, October 4, 1987.

I. PLANES, TRAINS, AND AUTOMOBILES

1. See also, things that rarely happen today, though there are a number of owners (Jerry Jones and Daniel Snyder come to mind) that would be prime candidates for player-related mockery.
2. Steve Delsohn, *Da Bears* (New York: Crown Archetype, 2010), 33.
3. Ibid., 28.
4. Ibid., 26–27.
5. Other names of interest to Bear fans include Glen Kozlowski, John Wojciechowski, and Mark Rodenhauser; all of whom would go on to make significant future contributions.
6. Flutie was soon traded to the New England Patriots. He was Ditka's most controversial personnel decisions—one that was almost universally panned in print and other media by Bears players. Said Dan Hampton in Steve Delsohn's book *Da Bears*, "With Flutie, I think Ditka was flailing at the piñata."
7. Norvell also coached this author, when the former was an assistant coach under Barry Alvarez at the University of Wisconsin (UW), and the latter was an unremarkable high school player from Indiana in the early 1990s and attended a UW football camp.

8. Which he also, incidentally, famously declared again when he took the head coaching job in Arizona, where he failed to make the playoffs.

9. Delsohn, *Da Bears*, 238.

10. Ibid.

11. They would famously lose to Ditka's Bears in the 1988 "Fog Bowl" playoff game, underneath a blanket of fog at Soldier Field.

12. Add "Egypt Allen" and "Guido Merkens" to an imaginary list of "Potential First and Middle Names of Future Children."

13. Bell was on the New York Jets' active roster in 1984.

14. Cross was actually a former Philadelphia Eagle, and his jersey number 27 was worn by a rotund replacement running back named Topper Clemons.

15. Also known as Kurt Warner's alma mater. Incidentally, Knapczyk used the money he made during the strike games to go back and get his bachelor's from Northern Iowa. Cool.

16. This is the comment that would have gotten Braman pilloried if he'd said it in 2014. Fortunately, for Braman, it was 1987.

17. If you're reading this after, say, the year 2020, "reality television" is a thing where they put supposedly real people in a bunch of unscripted supposedly real situations and just let the cameras capture what happens.

18. It's worth noting that in the 1980s, teams would bring in as many as 100 or more players for training camp, cutting many of them within the first few weeks. There were so many guys in camp that teams would routinely have to double up on jersey numbers in the preseason and often teams would have a guy in camp whose only job was to snap the ball to quarterbacks in individual drills. This is in contrast to today where there is a hard limit on the number of players that can be invited to an NFL training camp.

19. The punt invokes memories of Sean Landeta, as Merkens nearly misses his foot as he drops the ball. Landeta, of course, did this in a 1985 playoff game against Chicago in windy Soldier Field, missing his foot completely and leading to a Chicago touchdown.

20. This is shortly before he suggests that the replacement Bears should scrimmage the actual Bears. His performance on this telecast reminds me of that of the Fred Willard character in the mockumentary *Best In Show*, in that everything Bradshaw says is more ridiculous than the last thing he said. At one point he says, in reference to the cheerleaders, "They're pretty little girls aren't they? They sure do a lot of kicking and running around." Somewhere in the control truck a CBS producer tenders his resignation.

2. DIDN'T WE ALMOST HAVE IT ALL

1. I should note that I found out later that Bock actually made the Rochester Raiders on his own merits, so in reality, I was the only publicity stunt in the above scenario.

2. I'm still undecided as to which set of initials looks and sounds more ridiculous, but sometimes I verbally call the CIFL the "siffle" and am reminded how close that sounds to "syphilis."

3. It's no secret that I think the USFL was underrated, super-entertaining, and offered a unique spring football product. I wish that league hadn't folded.

4. The Detroit Lions and Houston Oilers would eventually adopt the run-and-shoot, to mixed success. The offense helped Oilers quarterback Warren Moon become a Hall of Famer, but neither team ever won a title with it.

5. Overtime brings with it a Chevrolet commercial in which a sports car is apparently driving on the surface of Mars while dodging 1980s-quality CGI fireballs that emerge from the ground, and another creepy Lowenbrau ballad, this time while guys skydive using rainbow-festooned parachutes. I really miss the 1980s.

3. FULL METAL JACKET

1. Although Seattle Seahawk and 2014 Super Bowl champion quarterback Russell Wilson is only 5'10".

2. I met Khayat when he was head coach of the Nashville Kats in the Arena Football League, and I was one of many players in town for a cattle-call open tryout. I remember him most for the giant cigar on which he chomped, while looking bored out of his mind.

4. WHO WILL YOU RUN TO?

1. These were the best. Being that it was the Midwest in the 1980s, these phones usually hung next to some kind of tacky "country" art like a tin cutout of a chicken.

2. The most horrific of which, in central Indiana, were the kind of mullets where the back of it would be "permed." I'm convinced this is the actual reason that Russia wanted to nuke us in the 1980s.

3. For me, this was running back Randy McMillian and kick returner Billy "White Shoes" Johnson, who was at the end of his career, was unbelievable friendly, and was almost smaller than me.

4. Aubrey Linne, a tall tight end who played one game with Baltimore in 1961.

5. It's unclear as to whether the jersey Linne was wearing was Fryar's *actual* jersey, though it did appear to be about two sizes too big for Linne, who sort of looks like what a kid looks like when he briefly puts on his dad's clothes.

6. Most recently, Fryar was pastor of a charismatic-sounding church (New Jerusalem House of God) in New Jersey, but was also implicated in an alleged mortgage scam of some kind in 2013.

7. Incidentally, Collins has one of the most jankety stances in modern NFL history. His feet are so wide and his left hand is out so far forward that his ass appears to be in danger of hitting the turf before the play even starts, and I wonder how he can effectively move laterally from a stance like this.

8. This is not a typo. Way to keep it classy, Miami. Somehow, the Arena Football League survived this gaffe.

9. Incidentally, this is the best version of the New England Patriots uniform in my opinion. Three fat stripes down the middle of the white helmet, white face mask, and Revolutionary minuteman snapping the football; white jersey with red numbers and blue accents, with red pants. This was a good look. It was replaced a few years later in the mid-1990s by a uniform that had a vaguely "U.S. Postal Service" look about it.

10. "N.F.L. TV Ratings Drop," *New York Times*, Oct. 6, 1987. http://www.nytimes.com/1987/10/09/sports/nfl-tv-ratings-drop.html.

11. Leonard Shapiro, "How Another Strike Can Be Avoided: Harmony, " *Athlon's Pro Football,* June 1987, 199.

12. James had clean-cut, frat boy good looks and the sort of Southern "aww-shucksiness" that made him perfect for this kind of role.

5. YO, BUM RUSH THE SHOW

1. Paul Zimmerman, "Left with an Empty Feeling,"*Sports Illustrated.* Oct. 12, 1987, 39.

2. Ibid., 40.

3. Ibid., 43.

4. NFL Films, *1988 Season Review,* 1989. In the same film, Cleveland quarterback Bernie Kosar is quoted saying, "I think they've done a good job in setting the rules up to protect quarterbacks. Injuries are part of the game . . . that's just part of football. Those things are going to happen." Kosar has since

publicly spoken of CTA-related symptoms. An injured Kosar was replaced in the lineup in 1988 by thirty-eight-year-old career Miami backup, Don Strock, whose Florida tan was so deep that he looked African American.

5. Greg Garber, "A Tormented Soul," ESPN.com, January 25, 2005. http://sports.espn.go.com/nfl/news/story?id=1972285.

6. Ibid.

7. Ibid.

8. Jackson is listed at 230 pounds, but looks much bigger, like 250 or 260. He looks like an earlier incarnation of Jerome Bettis. It seems like the Steelers have always had huge, effective backs. See also Barry Foster, and to a certain degree, for his time, Franco Harris, who was big if not physical.

9. *Athlon's Pro Football 1987 Annual*, 146.

10. Ibid.

11. Lansford kicked barefooted, which was totally a 1980s thing to do, given that by the mid-1990s, nobody was doing it anymore because people realized how ridiculous it was. Rich Karlis and Tony Franklin were the NFL's most famous barefooted kickers, which is amazing given that they kicked in Denver and Philly, respectively, which are both ice-and-snow-type NFL locales. I could see kicking barefoot in a domed stadium or in Miami, but not in Veterans Stadium in December.

12. McDonald was a power forward at USC.

13. In a piece of quintessentially 1980s/early-1990s trivia, White also appeared three times on the show *American Gladiators*, which was a campy paean to spandex and steroid use (which could also be said of the NFL in this era). He won all three times.

14. *Athlon's Pro Football 1987 Annual*, P68.

15. Ibid.

16. Tom Callahan, *The GM: A Football Life, a Final Season, and a Last Laugh* (New York: Three Rivers Press, 2007), 150.

6. WALL STREET: MONEY NEVER SLEEPS

1. My son, on the old red-jersey, gray-pants, red-helmet Atlanta Falcons uniform of the mid-1980s: "That is *so* fresh."

2. I swear, this is the last *Jerry Maguire* reference I'll put in, meaning I'll actually slip in about six more. I saw the film on my honeymoon with my new bride, so it will always have nostalgic vibes for me. I've also (full disclosure) seen it about 150 times since then.

3. Bill Saporito, "The Life of a $725,000 Scab," *Fortune*. October 26, 1987. Accessed online.

4. Hugo Lindgren, "The Lives They Lived," *The New York Times Magazine*, December 21, 2013.

5. Paul Zimmerman. *The Thinking Man's Guide to Pro Football* (New York: Simon and Schuster, 1984), 21.

6. Leonard Shapiro, "How Another Strike Can Be Avoided: Harmony." *Athlon's Pro Football*, 199.

7. Bill Saporito, "The Life of a $725,000 Scab," *Fortune*. October 26, 1987. Accessed online.

8. Ibid.

9. Ibid.

7. YOU KEEP ME HANGING ON

1. Some semipublicized drug arrests that are hopefully behind him, but which I choose not to dwell on here or in my interview with Reaves.

2. Not to mention team-supplied prescription painkillers, which may be the NFL's next large public-relations fiasco/challenge.

3. Nobody got more screwed by Indy's 1987 blockbuster trade for Eric Dickerson than Bentley, who may have been the best running back in the USFL and may have still been the best, most versatile, least–prima donna running back on the Colts even after Dickerson's arrival.

4. Reaves strikes me as the kind of guy who's almost always the coolest person in whatever group he's in, and probably also knows it.

5. Wheaton College is, incidentally, in Wheaton, Illinois (a well-heeled Chicago suburb), and is known in certain circles as being the "Harvard" of conservative Evangelical higher education, making it an odd place to launch a new professional football league.

6. Home to another seminal and quintessentially 1980s childhood memory for the author—watching WWF/E champion Hulk Hogan bodyslam and pin erstwhile 1980s villain the Iron Sheikh back when it was apparently totally okay to have wrestling villains based on ethnic differences, which makes me recall, somewhat wistfully, that "outrage" really wasn't a "thing" in the 1980s. Sigh.

8. STAND BY ME

1. Reilly, incidentally, went on to become the modern era's first rockstar sportswriter and whose stylistic offspring include, for better or worse, guys like Bill Simmons. Still, it should be noted that in a Rick Reilly–less world, I may

still be functionally illiterate, as his back-page *Sports Illustrated* column may have been the only thing I ever read between roughly 1986 and 1993.

2. The supplemental draft was most famously implemented for Herschel Walker when he left Georgia and for all of the players who migrated over from the folded USFL in 1986.

3. Michael Weinreb, *Bigger Than the Game* (New York: Gotham Books, 2010), ix–x.

4. Boz, in his "autobiography," referred to Butler as "my main guru and chief good ol' Tennessee boy."

5. Butler's accent and delivery has remained remarkably "Tennessee" in spite of the fact that he spent a decade in hipster Seattle, followed by another decade in rust-belt Pittsburgh.

6. Brian Bozworth with Rick Reilly, *The Boz* (New York: Doubleday, 1988), 233. Incidentally, if the 1980s represented the apex of crappily ghost-written and hastily conceived sports biographies, this book is the apex of that apex (in that the writing isn't at all crappy). I can't recommend it highly enough, as it's kind of pre-Reilly Reilly in that he's writing "as" someone else but he's really writing as Reilly.

7. Ibid., 232.

8. "Downtown" Julie Brown was another personality who seemed to literally vanish into the ether sometime during the mid-1990s.

9. Ibid.

10. The Ditka sweater, the Marv Levy flat-brimmed ball cap before it actually became hipster/bro-fashionable to wear them that way, and pretty much everything that Bum Phillips ever wore.

11. Like most football fans, I was addicted to this for a few years, but now I can see that it ruined most of my Sunday afternoons and also that the existence of it is ruining televised football.

12. As writers in the Bill Simmons era, we all just have to live with the fact that part of it involves trying to be more clever and funny than the last guy, which, in my opinion, makes for a really annoying product. Admission: I try to do it. Caveat: I think Simmons is truly clever and talented.

13. Kemp is the son of former NFL quarterback and prominent Republican politician Jack Kemp, who it seemed like was always almost the Republican nominee for president.

9. THE LAST EMPEROR

1. In 1987, you could buy a tiny car called a Subaru "Justy" for $5,500 brand new. Also, men's razor-blade commercials were way more erotic in

1987 . . . the subtext of all of them seemed to be, "If you use this Schick razor, the woman in the bedroom surrounded by billowing drapes will soon come into your bathroom to stroke the part of your cheek that doesn't have shaving cream on it, right before making love to you."

10. WITH OR WITHOUT YOU

1. Clancy is 6'7" and 250 pounds, and was a basketball player in college at Pittsburgh, where he did not play football. He was a third-round draft choice of the Phoenix Suns and averaged 11.5 points per game for the Billings Volcanos of the Continental Basketball Assocation (CBA) prior to making the switch to professional football. His son, Sam Clancy Jr., was a basketball standout at USC, and he also has a son named Selfopromotio, which I can only assume is Latin for "self promotion." It is also awesome.

2. Tom Callahan, *The GM: A Football Life, a Final Season, and a Last Laugh* (New York: Three Rivers Press, 2007), 150.

3. Bolden would go on to earn his doctor of ministry degree at Ashland Theological Seminary, and now does ministry full-time in Washington, D.C.

4. Walter went to college at Northern Michigan University (NMU), notable not only for being Steve Mariucci's alma mater, but also for the fact that it's in Michigan's upper peninsula, where it is winter for most of the calendar year. As such, the NMU football team plays its home games in a facility called the Youper Dome ("Youper" is a euphemism for those who live in the upper peninsula), which is a domed stadium made primarily of wood.

5. Bengals outside linebacker Toney Catchings had a similar arc. Though he only played in the three replacement games as an NFL player, the University of Cincinnati product would play productively for a decade in the Arena Football League.

6. Paul Daugherty, "Ex-Bengal Reggie Williams Fighting to Save His Leg," *USA Today* Sports. August 26, 2013. http://www.usatoday.com/story/sports/nfl/bengals/2013/08/25/reggie-williams-cincinnati/2697069/.

7. Ibid.

8. Ibid.

9. Ibid.

10. Bennett would go on to enjoy a longish career that included stints in the Arena Football League and the World League of American Football.

11. Mason played collegiately at Troy State and had stints in the USFL and with the Miami Dolphins, as well, which, in a sense, made him the perfect replacement running back in that he had had significant carries in pro games but wasn't yet old.

12. Not the same David Ward who would go on to write and direct bad sports movies, including an early-1990s football movie called *The Program*, which includes perhaps every imaginable football-related cliché, but which, like *Rocky IV*, is also oddly compelling and watchable in spite of its obvious crappiness.

13. Since coming to Cleveland in a 1985 trade with Detroit, Danielson suffered a torn rotator cuff, a dislocated shoulder, and a broken ankle.

14. Callahan, *The GM: A Football Life, a Final Season, and a Last Laugh*, 150.

15. Ibid.

16. In the commercial break that followed, there was an ad for Dristan nasal spray, in which the very 1980s medical cartoon silhouette was used, as though the viewer would have any trouble figuring out that nasal spray does indeed go up one's nose. I then learned that beef is "Real food, for real people."

17. NFL Films, *1988 Season Review*, DVD, 1989.

18. Ibid.

19. This was one of the worst instances of the "prevent" defense in NFL history, as the Bengals persisted in only rushing three defenders at Montana throughout the drive, allowing Montana ample time to pick apart the Bengals secondary. After the game, though, Wyche classily said to his mentor Bill Walsh, "I'm happy for you like I've never been."

20. Regarding the football gods and fickleness, a Cleveland running back, Stacy Driver, collapses in his stance and is carried off the field by trainers, a mere two minutes away from celebrating a nice run as a replacement player and an exceptional game. His replacement is Johnny Davis, who was working as a piano player in Cleveland's jazz clubs.

EPILOGUE

1. The game also featured three future NFL head coaches in Chicago's rookie quarterback Jim Harbaugh, reserve linebacker Ron Rivera, and Seattle tight end Mike Tice.

2. Surreal commercials: A holiday spot in which Taco Bell tries to package itself as "family" fare, and features a Brooklyn Tabernacle Choir-esque group singing a dramatic jingle about tacos. The fact that this happened makes me love 1987 even more. A Tom Wopat and John Schneider vehicle called *Christmas Comes to Willow Creek*, which involves, as far as I can tell, a semi-truck and lots of dialogue that happens on CB radios and was, no doubt, every bit as dreadful as it sounds. A Schick electric razor involving a guy sculpting a giant statue of a guy's face. Overall, there was still a fascination with the idea of the

cowboy. And it also seemed like James Garner appeared in nearly half of the commercials that aired. The undergirding ethic in 1980s advertising seemed to be that you can have it all and all your dreams can come true, whereas today's ethic is more cynical, more clever, but less hopeful.

3. To a certain segment, Olsen is better remembered as a cuddly, bearded, and neighborly character on *Little House on the Prairie*. But NFL fans remember the bad-assery he wrought as a member of the L. A. Rams' "Fearsome Foursome."

4. He would recover another fumble, by Tomczak, later in the quarter.

5. Payton recorded a music video and single, in conjunction with Kentucky Fried Chicken, entitled "Doin' It Right," which involved him singing and dancing in a Cosby sweater. It sold half a million copies and is exactly the sort of horrible piece of pop culture that I really want to own a copy of.

6. Military advertising was especially awesome in this era. "We're not a company, we're your country." There was also a great ad for "Contel Satellites" (?) starring Charlton Heston in a velour jogging suit, by a pool, and Smith Barney Investments, reminding us that they make money the old-fashioned way. They earn it.

7. The Redskins had a kicker named Ali Haji-Shiekh, who sounds like a 1980s pro wrestling heel.

8. He played the first few series with his chin strap unsnapped and just sort of dangling, uselessly, off his helmet.

9. Rodgers came out of South Carolina with a ton of hype and potential, but became something of a poster child for the NFL's cocaine problem in the 1980s (see also Manley, Dexter). After being jettisoned by New Orleans, he was resurrected in Washington.

10. The wind chill on the field was negative five; however, one Redskin equipment man wore a pair of 1980s (mid-thigh) polyester coaching shorts for the duration of the game—another source of entertainment for my boys. There's always one guy like this (shorts in any weather) on every team.

11. On work furlough from prison on a cocaine conviction.

12. Mike Richman, "Redskins Legacy: 1987 Replacement Team," Redskins.com, October 25, 2014, http://www.redskins.com/news-and events/article-1/Redskins-Legacy-1987-Replacement-Team/10c19faf-4e95-4111-839e-1696146aac7a

13. Ibid.

14. Ibid.

15. Other lyrics include "Body graceful. Body proud."

16. Kosar recently went public as a part of a large group of athletes who have admitted to dealing with symptoms related to chronic traumatic encephalopathy (CTE).

17. Cleveland's defense featured outside linebacker Clay Matthews Sr., whose long locks flowed from the back of his helmet, much like his son's do today. Matthews was a productive linebacker in the league for nearly twenty years, though never as flashy has his son.

18. Nattiel and his receiving counterparts, Mark Jackson and Vance Johnson, were nicknamed "The Three Amigos." Campy sports nicknames are a lost art (see also, The Steel Curtain, The Orange Crush, The Fearsome Foursome, The Smurfs).

19. Sanders torched cornerback Mark Haynes who was in press coverage. Williams noticed the press and the mismatch and threw a perfect rope up the sideline for an eighty-yard score.

20. It would be Smith's finest hour, as he would go on to start only nine games in an injury-plagued career that would end with the Dallas Cowboys in 1990—a season which saw him gain six yards rushing. In 2005, Smith was jailed for the distribution of cocaine.

BIBLIOGRAPHY

Athlon's Pro Football 1987 Annual, June 1987.

Bosworth, Brian, and Rick Reilly. *The Boz*. New York: Doubleday, 1988.

Callahan, Tom. *The GM: A Football Life, a Final Season, and a Last Laugh*. New York: Three Rivers Press, 2007.

Chicago Bears vs. Philadelphia Eagles. DVD. CBS Sports, 1987.

Cleveland Browns vs. Cincinnati Bengals. DVD. NBC Sports, 1987.

Cleveland Browns vs. New England Patriots. DVD. NBC Sports, 1987.

Daugherty, Paul. "Ex-Bengal Reggie Williams Fighting to Save His Leg." *USA Today Sports*, August 26, 2013. http://www.usatoday.com/story/sports/nfl/bengals/2013/08/25/reggie-williams-cincinnati/2697069/.

Def Jam Recordings. "Since 1984: Public Enemy Releases Debut Album 'Yo! Bum Rush the Show,'" 1987.

Delsohn, Steve. *Da Bears*. New York: Crown Archetype, 2010.

Garber, Greg. *A Tormented Soul*. ESPN.com. January 25, 2005. http://sports.espn.go.com/nfl/news/story?id=1972285.

Lindgren, Hugo. "The Lives They Lived." *The New York Times Magazine*.

"NFL TV Ratings Drop." *The New York Times*, October 6, 1987.

1988 Season Review. DVD. NFL Films, 1989.

Richman, Mike. "Redskins Legacy: 1987 Replacement Team." Redskins.com.

Saporito, Bill. "The Life of a $725,000 Scab." *Fortune*. October 26, 1987.

Shapiro, Leonard. "How Another Strike Can Be Avoided: Harmony." *Athlon's Pro Football*, June 1987, 199.

Seattle Seahawks vs. Chicago Bears. VHS. CBS Sports.

Seattle Seahawks vs. Detroit Lions. DVD. NBC Sports.

St. Louis Cardinals vs. San Francisco 49ers. DVD. CBS Sports.

30 for 30: Brian and the Boz. DVD. ESPN Original Entertainment, 2014.

30 for 30: From Elway to Marino. DVD. ESPN Original Entertainment, 2014.

Washington Redskins vs. Chicago Bears. VHS. CBS Sports.

Weinreb, Michael. *Bigger Than the Game*. New York: Gotham Books, 2010.

Zimmerman, Paul. "Left with an Empty Feeling." *Sports Illustrated*, October 12, 1987, 39–43

———. *The Thinking Man's Guide to Pro Football*. New York: Simon & Schuster, 1984.

INDEX

ABOUT THE AUTHOR

Ted Kluck is the award-winning author of over a dozen books. Ted's work has appeared in *ESPN the Magazine, Sports Spectrum Magazine,* and ESPN.com Page 2. A bimonthly column for *Sports Spectrum Magazine* entitled "Pro and Con" won the Evangelical Press Association award for best standing column in 2003. Ted is the author of *Robert Griffin III: Athlete, Leader, Believer* (2013) and collaborator for NFL Hall of Famer Jim Kelly on *Playbook for Dads* (2012).

Ted played a season of professional indoor football with the Battle Creek (Michigan) Crunch of the Continental Indoor Football League and lived to tell about it in *Paper Tiger: One Athlete's Journey to the Underbelly of Pro Football* (2007), part homage to George Plimpton and part gritty travelogue through the dingy arenas and bus trips that make up minor league football. This book was named a Michigan Notable Book for 2008, joining the ranks of such authors as Jim Harrison and Elmore Leonard.

Game Time: Inside College Football (2007) is a collection of scene pieces and interviews that Ted put together from all levels of college football. Included are features on a coach who tried to integrate the football program at Jackson State, a walk-on at the University of Michigan, a Heisman Trophy winner committed to rebuilding the inner city of New Orleans, and the annual NFL meat market that is the Senior Bowl in Mobile, Alabama.

Ted's first book, *Facing Tyson: Fifteen Fighters, Fifteen Stories,* features interviews with fifteen men who fought Mike Tyson. Ted met these men in their homes, their gyms, and their streets, providing a fascinating look at this savage sport and the men who populate it. The book was published internationally through Mainstream Publishing (Edinburgh, Scotland).

Ted has played professional indoor football, coached high school football, trained as a professional wrestler, served as a missionary, and taught writing courses at the college level. He lives in Grand Ledge, Michigan, with his wife Kristin and sons Tristan and Maxim, where he writes, teaches, and speaks.